the Healing Breath

Also by Jack Angelo

*Your Healing Power: A comprehensive guide to channelling your
healing energies*

*The Spiritual Healing Handbook: How to develop your healing powers
and increase your spiritual awareness*

(with Jan Angelo)

*The Distant Healing Handbook: How to send healing to people,
animals, the environment and global trouble spots*

About the author

JACK ANGELO has been a teacher and writer in the fields of energy
medicine and natural spirituality since the mid 1980s. The breath and
breathing are key aspects of this work. He lectures and gives work-
shops to health-care professionals and the general public, both in the
UK and abroad. For ten years Jack was a tutor for the NFSH Healing
Trust. Having worked with Native American medicine teachers, Jack
sees indigenous and shamanic wisdom as the origin of all spiritual
traditions and a gateway through which we can access healing and
spirituality. His books have been translated into sixteen languages.

the Healing Breath

How to use the power of
breathing to heal, reduce stress
and improve wellbeing

Jack Angelo

piatkus

PIATKUS

First published in Great Britain in 2010 by Piatkus as *The Self-Healing Handbook*
This edition published in 2017 by Piatkus

Copyright © 2010 by Jack Angelo

1 3 5 7 9 10 8 6 4 2

The moral right of the author has been asserted.

A CIP catalogue record for this book
is available from the British Library.

ISBN 978-0-7499-5294-5

Text designed and set by Paul Saunders
Illustrations by Rodney Paull

Printed and bound in Great Britain by
Clays Ltd, St Ives plc

Papers used by Piatkus are from well-managed forests
and other responsible sources.

MIX
Paper from
responsible sources
FSC® C104740

Piatkus
An imprint of
Little, Brown Book Group
Carmelite House
50 Victoria Embankment
London EC4Y 0DZ

An Hachette UK Company
www.hachette.co.uk

www.improvementzone.co.uk

Contents

Acknowledgements

I would like to thank Gill Bailey, for her constant encouragement and guidance during the creation of the book; my editors Claudia Dyer and Charlotte Ridings, for further creative guidance, and the whole Piatkus team; Jan Angelo, for her creative input and patient review of the manuscript; and my teaching students and workshop participants over the years, who have made so many positive contributions to the creation of this manual of self-healing.

List of exercises

List of illustrations

Introduction

The future has arrived

In the 1930s, the inspired mystic and healer Alice Bailey warned that centuries of cultural conditioning, and especially social and psychological conditioning, have created large populations of spiritually dysfunctional people who struggle to realise their full potential and discover who they really are. The solution to these problems, Alice Bailey predicted, would be the widespread use of carefully designed breathing exercises, with their ability to reorganise and readjust a person's energetic constitution and so bring about self-healing. *The Healing Breath* announces that that future has arrived!

The healing power of the breath

We all breathe all the time. Breathing is that simple. Yet the secret of life and healing, contained within the breath, is almost always remote from our everyday awareness. Being aware of a person's breathing has always been an integral part of my healing practice, and it has been a large focus in my work with groups. As a practitioner, I sense how the availability of the healing *life force* to another person is enhanced through conscious breathing. Further, the availability of the healing life force is proportional to a person's awareness of the sacred source of energy within the breath. This is crucial for our own healing and for those with whom we may work. The special techniques presented in *The Healing Breath* offer you the opportunity to strengthen your link with the sacred life force through the breath. The natural side effects will be healing on all levels of your being, enhanced good health, energetic balance, a new self-awareness, heightened consciousness and the ability to help others. You will have discovered that the secret of life and healing is the breath.

Remembering the breath of life

The window where I write looks out on a lake, with a mountain rising up behind it. Today, there is a commotion down in the car park. People are laughing and chatting together, shaking hands and donning boots. Once a month, a group of walkers meets here for a hike into the mountains. A man stands up and thumps his chest. 'Smell that mountain air!' he exclaims, and the women laugh. My attention is drawn to a bent figure, leaning on a stone wall and watching them from a distance. I recognise the outline; it is Charlie, a friend for over twenty years.

When I first moved to South Wales in the early 1980s, Charlie showed me the mountain walks and pathways. He was a retired miner, broad and strong, with keen brown eyes that studied you from under the peak of his cap. In those days, Charlie's laboured breath was just becoming noticeable. 'It's my chest,' he'd mutter, grinning as if he'd at last met up with the miner's traditional adversary – emphysema. Charlie would talk about his days underground and how miners valued fresh air. There was nothing like the first breath when they came up from the pit. On our walks together, Charlie savoured the scents of the mountain: the smell of the sheep, a rotting carcass, a bank of heather, the tang of iron in a rushing stream.

Now, twenty years later, Charlie's breath comes in gasps. A few steps exhaust him with the effort of breathing. On this sunny spring day, with the help of a stick, he makes it to a gate to watch the walkers set off on their hike. I treasure my walks with Charlie. Without saying anything, he reminded me how nature calls us to embrace the breath of life as it comes to us, unconditionally.

The Breath of Unity

The breath carries the life force, so the breath is our moment-by-moment connection with the source of life and all healing energies – which can be called the Source, or God. Through the simple and natural act of breathing we can become more aware of this *Breath of Unity* and open ourselves to the flow of healing energies. This is why conscious, mindful breathing is integral to self-healing and all other forms of therapy.

Breathing is our moment-by-moment link with life itself. When we breathe we take in the energy of our surroundings, as well as physical substances such as air, so that breathing is an interaction between our inner emotional, mental and spiritual selves and our surroundings. Thus, just as it affects our physical body, our breathing also affects the emotional, mental and spiritual aspects of ourselves. Therefore it is vital that we know how to breathe effectively at all levels of our being. The first step in self-healing through conscious breathing is to become aware of the breath as a function of our connection with the Source. This book will show you how the breath is our pathway to well-being, to balance, to mental clarity, to the absence of stress, and to a deep awareness of the gift of life.

Over centuries, as the words and concepts relating to the breath and breathing were absorbed by Western cultures, they became adapted to suit various religious and philosophical agendas. Consequently, today there is some confusion about the meaning of many of these terms. In English, for example, the word 'spirit' can refer to the individual soul as well as one aspect of the Christian triune vision of the Source: the Holy Spirit. In addition, spirit is defined as the force that animates the body of a living being. For the sake of clarity, in this book, Spirit (with a capital 's') signifies an aspect of the Source while the term 'spirit' refers to the animating energy of the Source.

Lessons I've learnt about the breath and breathing

We don't have to remind our body to breathe; if something prevents us from breathing, our brain alerts us to take steps to breathe. In my years as a healer and practitioner of natural spirituality and shamanism, I have discovered that this necessity to breathe and to join with all other living, breathing beings in this way can be a basis for finding meaning in life itself.

Like most of us, the beginning of my life is enshrined in family stories. Apparently, when I was pulled from my mother's body by a pair of large steel forceps, I was held aloft by my ankles, head down. My response to this was to take a gulp of air and howl. This meant that I did not receive the customary smack on the behind, which, in those days, was designed to initiate you into breathing. We acknowledge that human life, once we are outside our mother's womb, begins with that first breath. What we don't think about is that the rest of our life, in a sense, will be about how we breathe.

I remember as a small child being frightened by the campaign to eradicate diphtheria. This is an acute contagious disease where bacterial toxins cause serious inflammation of the heart and nervous system. According to the graphic posters of the time, diphtheria also caused a membrane to grow across your throat so that, eventually, you could not breathe. 'Do you want your child to suffer that?' the caption thundered. My father disapproved of vaccination, but I never caught diphtheria. Then, in the middle of a severe winter, I contracted measles. The water pipes in our house burst and my bout of measles turned into pneumonia. I stopped breathing a number of times, but my only recollection of the experience is of swimming in a soundless sea of swirling colours. I was out of my body. I was being looked after. During the experience of pneumonia, and my inability to breathe, I was learning about the preciousness of the breath and its link with ill-health. I was also being reminded of my existence before the breath, and that I exist with the breath and, on some level, without it.

Years later, at school, I developed a love for long-distance running. I found that I ran best when I coordinated my breathing with the rhythmic beat of my feet on the ground. Breathing responds to rhythm. After school, judo training showed me how to use the breath to overcome the effects of my childhood illness to 'develop a strong body and a calm mind'. Through judo I discovered how the breath was linked to thought. Fear causes people to lose control of their breathing, whereas control of the breath creates a sense of calm, strength, and confidence. I have not forgotten the words of my instructor: 'When you need to be relaxed and serene, breathing is the key. When you need a clear head, breathing is the key. When you want to act quickly and efficiently, breathing is the key.' Sometimes, once a judo throw was mastered, the accompanying breath control allowed me to enter a space where thinking disappeared. I did not know it then, but this was the meditative state to which all forms of breath work and bodywork can lead.

My early childhood in the Gloucestershire countryside opened my heart and mind to the wonders of the natural world, giving me a lifelong interest in natural spirituality and shamanism. I have been fortunate to work with Native American medicine people, such as Wallace Black Elk, and to learn about Native American practices where conscious breathing is a feature of healing, chant, ritual and ceremony. There is an important place in all indigenous spiritual practice for simply being still. Some call this meditation. I have always found that the types of meditation that attract me are those linked to breathing, chanting, and movement (you will find some simple but effective meditation methods in the book). But, most of all, I enjoy walking in nature. Here, my breathing becomes slow and steady, my mind is stilled and immersion in the natural world induces a trance-like, meditative state where I feel quite safe and can walk without thinking about it.

I lived for a while with an Indian couple in London, and this sparked an interest in yoga. This ancient system of physical and mental exercise is based on the science of breath – *pranayama* – named after the Sanskrit word for the life force, prana. Since the life force has a central place in *The Healing Breath*, yoga practitioners will find much to interest them here.

Energy and the breath

Energy is the fundamental substance of nature, continually trans-
ferred between all its parts, including human beings. It is the process
that initiates all change. Energy has many physical forms, such as the
heat released when we metabolise food in our body, or the electricity
generated by a turbine. Energy also has many *subtle* forms, such as the
life force that animates living things and those used in self-healing,
hands-on and distant healing. Subtle energies travel faster than, or
just above the speed of light, and one of the properties associated with
their high vibratory speed is that subtle energies can travel within
oneself or to another person, being, landscape or situation, at any
distance, in an instant.

The life force and the breath

As well as carrying gases, such as oxygen and carbon dioxide, breath
is the agency for transferring the subtle energy of the life force, present
in air, to every cell in our body, via the blood. The life force is one of
many subtle energies that together create the subtle energetic base
for all life. Through our breathing, we absorb the life force; it circulates throughout every level of our being; and then we breathe it
out into the universe. In this way, the breath also unites us with all
other beings.

Subtle sensing

We know that the animating life force leaves a living thing at death,
for only the inanimate shell of its body remains. Even so, for much of
the time we live without being conscious of the subtle aspects of life.
Yet, as part of our being, we possess the ability to sense these subtle
aspects. Subtle sensing is a normal and natural way of sensing – we
just tend to stop using this ability as we grow out of early childhood.
It is sometimes referred to as the 'sixth sense'. Subtle sensing ranges
from intuitive knowledge to consciously or unconsciously sensing the
vibratory quality of energy. For example, when you enter a room you

may sense its atmosphere. The atmosphere comprises its energy field and many of the incidents that took place in it.

Since all matter is energy, everything and everyone has an energy field (also known as the *aura*) around them: the emanation of their specific energies. Some people, on meeting someone, are immediately able to sense the state of mental, emotional, or physical well-being of that individual. In such cases, subtle sensing means the ability to pick up and interpret the energetic information of another person's energy field.

As well as via our 'sixth sense', we are able to sense subtle energies via the palms of our hands. This is an ability that a novice healer first learns about. Healing energy, for example, may be sensed by the palms and interpreted as heat, cold, or sensations such as tingling. There is a direct link between the rhythm of the breath and a person's subtle sensing ability: the fuller and deeper the breath, the greater is our awareness of the subtle aspects of life. Most of the exercises in the book will thus help you rediscover and develop your subtle sensing and this will happen quite simply through practice.

The scope of this book

The concept of the breath as a direct pathway to self-healing and the sacred is explored in this book. My discoveries are based on my twenty-five years of experience with individuals and groups, through the practice of healing. We begin the exploration with recovering aspects of what we once knew about the breath and breathing, moving on to the physicality of the breath, and then looking at how subtle energies and the subtle energy of the life force support all physical life.

The Healing Breath will show you how to use your own breathing rhythm to:

- Enhance your ability to self-heal

- Breathe effectively and improve your posture

- Relax

- Ensure good digestion and sound sleep

- Relieve symptoms of stress and anxiety
- Bring emotional and mental calm
- Communicate effectively (essential for all those who use the voice in a professional setting, such as speakers, actors, broadcasters)
- Increase your energy levels
- Achieve energetic and physical balance
- Clear the system of negative energies
- Absorb positive energies
- Ensure protection from negative energies
- Expand your mind
- Achieve mental focus
- Express your true self via the breath
- Achieve your creative potential
- Prepare for healing or other therapeutic work
- Align yourself with the sacred
- Attune yourself to the natural world
- Access intuitive guidance
- Provide a time-honoured method for meditation

How to use this book

Each chapter includes simple breath and bodywork practices that you can do by yourself or with others. In addition, you will also be introduced to special exercises for self-healing, healing others, or simply for enhancing your daily life and well-being. Though you might want to begin by looking at certain topics, I suggest that you start by working with the basic themes of the first few chapters, including the exercises on subtle energetic hygiene at the end of Chapter 3. Regular practice of these essential exercises will ensure that it becomes second nature to take care of yourself. Once this is in place, you can explore the other topics in this book in any order that appeals to you.

The exercises encourage you to get to know your body through compassionate, non-judgemental observation of your body, becoming aware of feelings and sensations that you may not have noticed before. Paying complete attention to your body in this way, as you practise each exercise, allows you to be truly present – a state similar to the early stages of meditation.

To get the most out of your breathing exercises:

- Try to find a quiet place, inside or outdoors, for your practice.

- Sit or stand in a comfortable position, with your spine straight. A comfortable standing posture can be just as effective as sitting, resulting in a relaxed body and a relaxed mind, where you are able to observe how your body is feeling, how you are breathing, and what is going on around you, without becoming distracted by your observations.

- Breathe through your nose whenever possible.

- Close your eyes or choose something in your surroundings on which you can gently focus.

- Develop a passive yet confident and positive attitude, and enjoy the feelings of detachment from stress that come with effective breathing practice.

Some of the exercises suggest working with a partner. These will give you the added benefit of sharing and comparing experiences. It can be very useful to receive the encouragement and perspective of someone else. The book is ideal for group work and lends itself to the creation of a breathing course under the supervision of an experienced practitioner (see Web Resources for further information). However, I suggest that you do not practise more than three exercises in a single session. This keeps each session simple, allowing you to carefully study each exercise and appreciate your reactions. It is also important not to hyperventilate through being overenthusiastic while practising your exercises!

The power of intention

It has been shown by many researchers, including Dr Larry Dossey (author of *Healing Beyond the Body: Medicine and the Infinite Reach of the Mind*), that the intention behind anything and everything we do has a bearing on the outcome of the process. For this reason, make sure that you understand the aim of an exercise before you begin practising it and set your mind to complete it successfully. Your positive intention gives mental and emotional power to your physical actions and empowers you to remain open to whatever outcome you are presented with when doing an exercise.

By remaining unconditional and open-minded to the outcome of the exercise, you acknowledge the fact that you are a spiritual being and that your higher self dictates the activities of the healing, balancing and energising force. Your needs are not an isolated condition of the body, but an expression of the total you. This means that you cooperate with your body consciousness, rather than manipulate it. A relaxed attitude of acceptance about an outcome allows you to discover, or experience, the unexpected.

Keep a journal

You may find it useful, as well as fun, to keep a healing journal. In it you can keep a record of each breathing exercise with which you work, and document any changes you notice in yourself as a result. You can also record what you have noticed about your breathing on any given day. This could include the strength and quality of your breathing and what events, circumstances, thoughts and emotions seem to affect it. You may not always want to use words – try using drawings and making images too.

Keeping your healing journal will gradually put you back in touch with what our ancestors once knew about the breath and breathing. The exercises will help you rediscover what you intuitively know about the healing and unifying power of the breath and you will soon be able to create your own self-healing programme.

There may be days when you do not have the time or space to practise an exercise, but there is something you can do to maintain your conscious link with the Breath of Unity. Simply pause wherever you are, close your eyes, and breathe four to six slow, relaxed breaths while focusing on your breathing. Perform this conscious breathing as often as you can, up to six times in any 24 hours. Remember, it is the breath as carrier of the life force that makes it the Breath of Unity. This breath of sacred unity is fundamental to all the self-healing exercises in the book.

Chapter 1

What we once knew: a history of the breath

From the beginning

Life seems, mysteriously, to begin and end with the breath. From the first recorded observations of our very distant ancestors, found painted on the walls of caves, we know that breathing and the breath have probably always fascinated humans, since before they set off on their migrations to every part of the Earth. Later, the ancient Hebrews described how the Creator formed the first human (*'adam*) from the dust of the earth (*'adamah*) and then breathed the breath of life (*ruach*) into his nostrils. It was this sacred breath of life that transformed dust into a living being (Genesis 2:7).

Six thousand years ago, the ancient Egyptians detected that the breath seemed to actually carry life with it as a force they called *ka*. For the Egyptians, the key to understanding the origin of this force was the key to life itself: the *ankh*. The *ankh* was depicted as a cross-shaped key topped with a loop that could be held by the hand. It was a symbol of life, before, during, and after death. It therefore represents an ancient understanding of life as a force with its origin outside of the physical space–time frame. Much later, Coptic Christians, who were almost certainly influenced by Egyptian spiritual concepts, also used the *ankh* to symbolise life after death.

Qi

Two and a half thousand years ago, another civilisation was investigating the life force and self-healing. Practitioners of Traditional Chinese Medicine called the mysterious force *qi* or *chi*. The earliest way of writing *qi* consisted of three wavy lines representing the emanation of the breath (as clearly seen on a cold day, for example). Some ancient Chinese people believed that *qi* had a spiritual origin and conveyed a spiritual force that animated the whole universe. Others considered *qi* to be a universal force that was physical, although unseen, like the wind. Both groups understood that *qi* was taken in by the body during the process of breathing. It was then circulated round the body, and finally exhaled out into the universe to be made available to other beings.

In the Chinese system of exercises known as *Taiji* (t'ai chi), the practitioner seeks to accumulate *qi*, which is then circulated throughout the subtle energy body. The *qi* may then be consciously used as a source of power: to self-heal, to enhance life activities or for self-defence. Practitioners of *Taiji*, and various martial and defensive arts, also find their senses are enhanced the more they accumulate *qi*, and their balance and coordination improve too.

Japanese martial art and healing traditions

China's neighbour, Japan, soon adopted both the physical and spiritual versions of life force theory, calling it *ki* (the Japanese pronunciation of *qi*). This word and concept then appeared in terms such as *genki*, meaning healthy, and *byouki*, meaning sick. In the Japanese martial art of aikido, the word can be translated as 'the way (*do*) of harmonising your *ki* with the *ki* of your opponent'. Most energy and healing systems that incorporate the word ki, such as reiki, assert that it is possible to harness this special 'life force' energy in the lower abdomen, in the *subtle body* (the human subtle body and its energies are described in Chapter 3).

In both the Chinese and Japanese traditions, the profound physiological changes that enable special martial arts skills are developed through breathing exercises, deep relaxation and meditation practices that all aim to cultivate and store the life force energy (*qi* or *ki*).

Prana and breathing meditation

As I mentioned in my Introduction, most who have studied yoga will have come across the Sanskrit term *prana*. *Prana* also refers to the life force, a subtle energy in air that is brought into the body by the breath. The term was first recorded in the Upanishads, the great Indian teaching scriptures, the earliest of which date back to around 400 BCE. According to yogic philosophy, the breath, or air, is merely the vehicle for conveying *prana* to all levels of our being. Since *prana* carried life, it was more important to living beings than air. Yoga is designed to work with this enriching and healing life force, and many who practise yoga are introduced to *pranayama*, the science of breath and breathing.

According to pranic science, there are three main channels through which the subtle energy of *prana* travels. These are the central channel, which is aligned with the spine, and a channel on either side of the central channel, which convey incoming and outgoing energies respectively. These three main channels are linked to a vast network of finer channels within the subtle body of a person. Those who studied pranic science were the first to identify how the life force vibrated at a slower rate, thus becoming energetically 'denser', as it permeated down from its spiritual origins to the level of the physical body. Yoga still recommends the practice of breathing meditation because it is considered that the physical body becomes energetically less dense (vibrates at a faster rate) through meditation based on the person's breath. Breathing meditation allows the intake of more life force (*prana*) that, in turn, further reduces the relative density of the body. As this is reduced, the meditator is able to absorb increasingly finer grades of *prana*, providing an ever stronger link with the spiritual levels of being.

The Indian avatar Sathya Sai Baba counsels that, although there are many types of *pranayama*, the simplest (those that do not involve holding the breath for more than ten seconds) are the best for people living today and have the power to balance both mind and body. Practising any type of *pranayama* with the use of a mantra (a series of special Sanskrit sounds) is considered effective for mental transformation, while practising *pranayama* without using a mantra is effective for enhancing the body and its physical systems.

The transmission of spiritual power

The Brihadaranyaka Upanishad records the use of the breath to transmit *prana*, in the form of power and authority, from a patriarch to his successor, a practice probably derived from the methods used by gurus to initiate their students. Here, the breath is blown upon the person, usually on the face or head, but also on the centre of the chest or other parts of the body. Sometimes the transmissive breath was conveyed through sound syllables, such as a mantra. In every case, however, the person received *prana* that had been enhanced by its circulation through the physical and subtle levels of the authority figure or teacher. The receiver is thus considered to have been given an energy symbolising the gift of sacred succession. The transmission of power in this way, by shamans and holy people, has been noted by anthropologists in cultures all over the world.

The use of the breath to transmit power or knowledge is also recorded in the Christian Gospel of John. Here, the great teacher Jesus blows upon his disciples, with the words: 'Receive the Holy Spirit' (John 20:22). The text suggests that Jesus, behaving like many shamans, teachers and prophets down through time, was able to transmit divine power to his followers by breathing forcefully on them.

The language of breathing – breath, Spirit and the sacred

In the Near East of two thousand years ago, there seems to have been an understanding that healing, spiritual power and the life force were energies carried on the breath. Further, that these were divine energies which could be transmitted by a spiritually evolved person via the breath. Perhaps this is why the canonical records show that Jesus used the term 'Holy Breath', or 'Holy Spirit' more than any other reference to the presence of God. Thus, while our breath connects us to the physical world of air, the atmosphere and all that breathes, it also connects us to the creative breath and the presence of the divine.

Another definition of Spirit as spiritual power, or presence, occurs in the Gospel of Luke, which tells the story of the old priest Zechariah. Zechariah is standing by the sanctuary altar, about to offer incense, when the angel Gabriel appears and foretells the remarkable birth of a son to him and his barren wife. The son will turn out to be John the Baptist, who will later proclaim the presence of Jesus in the world. Even before John is born, says the angel, he will be filled with the Holy Spirit: the 'spirit and power of Elijah' (Luke 1:15–17). Here is a clear recognition, by people of that time, that great healers, prophets and teachers were imbued with, and exhibited, spiritual power.

The concept that the breath not only had a spiritual origin, but was a living exemplar of the sacred, is found throughout the ancient Middle Eastern, Greek and Roman worlds. The Hebrew word *ruach* can be translated as spirit, soul, or breath, while in the Aramaic of first-century Palestine, *rucha* translates as spirit, breath, wind and air. Here, as in Hebrew, the Semitic root sound *CH* indicates the breath of life. This root begins the name of the first woman, mentioned in Genesis – Chava (Eve). It also occurs in the Hebrew word *chaim*, life.

In Western traditions, the words for breath and soul are, again, related. The ancient Greek equivalent of *ruach* was *pneuma*, meaning spirit or breath of life. The Greek word *psyche* (soul) derives from the same root as the verb *psychein* (to breathe). The Latin of ancient Rome has the feminine word *anima* (the Spirit within) which has the same root as the word *animus* (wind). The English word 'spirit' comes from *spiritus*, the Latin for the breathing soul, courage and the vigour of life.

In the Welsh poetic tradition of the ancient Celtic world, the feminine noun *awen* is used to describe the divine inspiration of the bard. *Awen* and the Welsh word *awel* (breeze) are derived from the same root, *wel*, to blow. *Awen* is the breath of inspiration, or the breath of the divine that gives inspiration. In the Druidic spiritual tradition, with its roots deep in ancient Welsh culture and poetry, the breath and the whole natural world embody the concept of divine inspiration and so occupy a central place in Druid belief and sacred practice. This Celtic concept gives us a clue to the meanings behind the English word 'inspiration' (from Latin, *inspirare*, meaning to breathe in). Like life itself, we are able to access inspiration from the spiritual Source via the breath.

A signpost to the sacred

From her deep intuitive understanding, the female visionary and mystic Hildegard of Bingen (1098–1179) described God as the One Breath, to which everything returns. With each breath, Hildegard declared, we are breathing in God. With her mystical vision she saw all beings living in a sacred, breathing cosmos.

When Europeans came into contact with the native inhabitants of America, they found it difficult to believe that the Native American nations already had an advanced concept of God. In Lakota, for example, God is called *Wakhan Tanka*, where *wakhan* describes anything that is sacred or that is related to the spiritual dimension of life. For the Lakota nation, the breath of any being is considered *wakhan*, or sacred. The meaning of *tanka* ranges from 'big' to anything greater than we can comprehend. Thus, the nearest translation of *Wakhan Tanka* is 'Great Spirit'. But, like the words generated in the ancient Old World, these Lakota terms point to a spiritual concept that is too vast to be totally encapsulated in words, and too elusive to be captured by them. I think this is why one of my old Native American teachers preferred the term 'Great Mystery': the something or someone from which he was never separate. Interestingly, this teacher used his breath to transmit power, or even a teaching, especially in the purification (sweat) lodge ceremony.

Our very brief trip around the planet, to some of the roots of human ideas about the breath, reveals a remarkable coherence. From ancient times the concept of a life-giving force within the breath has been used by healers all over the world, consciously or unconsciously, in order to achieve optimal well-being in individuals, through opening and gaining access to the subtle energies of healing. Throughout all the different cultures and traditions, there is a clear link between the breath, air, life itself, the force beyond, before and after life, the force that enables life, and the source of life. Breathing and the breath presents us, or even confronts us, with its role as a signpost to the sacred.

The mystery of the breath

As we have mentioned, air not only contains oxygen, vital to brain function and physical life, but also the vital life force of subtle energy that animates the body. We are created as an aspect of the Source, to manifest divine Oneness. To do this we use a physical body and a personality. The individual soul creates the template for the body, including the brain, at a subtle level, and it is from this level that all Earthly life takes form and animation. Life is planned and begins at a spiritual, or subtle, level. This is why the life force is a subtle energy and why it is crucial to our own healing.

Our first intake of air is a union of the spiritual and the physical realms. When we take in the life force in this way, we signal that we have come to breathe the same breath as our ancestors did and to be a part of Earth life for a while. At the end of our journey, we give out our last breath to those we leave behind and to those who will follow. This last exhalation frees us from physicality and returns us to the spiritual realm from which we came. In between birth and death is life, filled with wonder and mystery. This mystery, like the Great Mystery my former teacher spoke of, is not something strange or something one should fear; rather, it is a celebration of a wonder that is beyond the comprehension of the mind yet always present in the heart.

Like many spiritual teachers, Sufi master Hazrat Inayat Khan (1882–1927) taught that 'life's mystery lies in the breath'. Part of the mystery of the breath is that every time we exhale, we breathe out part of our essence, which then returns to the rest of the universe. Then, each time we inhale, we breathe in the essence of the Source. In this way, we are constantly in touch with the divine and continuously replenishing the spirit, or essence, of the Source through the Breath of Unity.

Furthermore, we can see each breathing cycle as a metaphor for the cycle of life. As we inhale, the soul (spirit) enters into the physical world. The pause before the out-breath can be seen as the impact of the soul coming into the physical world, animating the body at birth. As we exhale, the soul leaves the physical world. The pause before the next in-breath can be seen as the impact of the soul leaving the body at the end of life.

It seems, then, that engaging with the breath, with spirit, wind and air, can carry us from one reality to another. Finding our home in the breath puts us at the balanced centre point between the spiritual and Earthly realms. Here in this balanced state of breathing, we rediscover the empowerment that energises our individual existence and the life of our community and brings healing to both.

Beginning to breathe

To begin to breathe effectively again means remembering what we only *seem* to have lost – our connection with the Source. Our relationship with our breathing can be seen as a statement about our relationship with the Source and our higher self, or who we really are. We know that, whereas earlier cultures and specific traditions have maintained a knowledge and practice of relating the breath to self-healing (and spirituality), Western culture has virtually abandoned this relationship. We have either forgotten it or ignored it and this is demonstrated by the poor breathing techniques of most people. Human history shows that we once knew that we were multidimensional beings, and that the breath and breathing nourished us on our emotional, mental and spiritual levels, as well as in our physical bodies. Thus, effective breathing is essential for receiving and maintaining total health.

We start this course in recovery and remembrance by finding out how you are breathing at this moment. Without judgement or anticipation, let's try simply breathing.

EXERCISE 1

Simply breathing

How do you breathe right now? You are about to discover the most important self-healing tool you will ever need to enhance your awareness of yourself and life around you and to expand

exercise continues ▶

your consciousness of the same. This is simply breathing. You will learn how to use this tool as you make your way through each of the exercises in the book. This first exercise helps you develop breath awareness and allows you to celebrate your relationship with your body, your breath and so, ultimately, with the Source.

- Sit or lie comfortably.

- Close your eyes (this sends a signal to your mind that you are present to yourself and thus detaching from external stimulation). Allow your mind to rest on your breath.

- Notice your body breathing in and breathing out. Notice your body moving in time to this breathing. Your chest and abdomen rise and fall; they rise on the in-breath and fall on the out-breath.

- Let your body breathe how it wants.

- Enjoy the feeling of your body breathing. Enjoy the rhythm of your body breathing.

- Enjoy the opportunity to be with your breathing and your body in this special way.

- Remain with your body and your breathing for as long as you want.

- When you feel ready, open your eyes, wiggle your toes, and stretch gently before standing.

You may be surprised at how much time has elapsed. Perhaps you were relaxed enough to drift into a gentle healing sleep. Your account of this exercise could be your first entry in your healing journal. You could ask yourself questions like: Were you able to rest on your breath? What did you notice about your body and your breathing? Did you find the experience enjoyable? What else did your breathing tell you? Use this as an assessment exercise when you first start working with the book.

The wisdom of the breath

The Breath of Unity connects us with the wisdom of the soul. When you are relaxing after a breathing exercise, allow the wisdom of your breath to teach you. On any particular day, your breath has a message for you if you take a few moments to listen. Here are some of the many things my breath has taught me:

- If we do not breathe, we are dead. Therefore we attend to what is most necessary in life.

- We cannot hold our breath for ever. It is best not to hoard anything: there is always enough. We can be generous with what we have: there is always the promise of the next breath.

- Erratic breathing is not good for health. Be alert to the harmful effects of stress and modern, fast-paced lifestyles.

- Breathing should be deep rather than shallow. Similarly, we should plunge into life and seek the depths of things, not remain simply skimming the surface.

You might like to take a moment to write in your journal what your breath has taught you.

We are now ready to look at how breathing actually works, the state of your own breathing, and the functioning of your own breathing-related systems.

Chapter *2*

Breathing: back to basics

Breath and physical life

Like Hazrat Khan, Lama Anagarika Govinda (1898–1985), the European founder of the Tibetan Buddhist Arya Maitreya Mandala,
described breath as the key to the mystery of life – to that of the body
as well as that of the Spirit. Breathing is one of a range of natural
rhythms that occur throughout the cosmos and all natural rhythms are
about some form of energy exchange. Where, and how, did we learn to
breathe? Part of the mystery of breathing is how, on leaving the liquid
world of amniotic fluid in our mother's womb, we instinctively begin
to breathe air through the nose and mouth, via the movement of our
diaphragm.

Unless we suffer from a respiratory disorder, we are not forced to
think about our breathing. Just like the circulation of blood, breathing
is automatic, under the control of the autonomic nervous system. Like
the other systems of the body, such as the endocrine system, we do not
have to ask our breathing apparatus to keep going since it is a function
of the coordinated living body.

When we are upset our breathing rate and heartbeat increase, due
to the secretion of adrenaline. By controlling our breathing and
calming it, we can regain the balance of our mind and emotions. This
sends a message to the adrenal glands, which sit just above the
kidneys, to stop secreting adrenaline so that our breath and heartbeat are further calmed. By the simple act of controlling our breathing,

we are better able to cope with stress. That said, in any situation, our breathing can be one of the first things we notice about ourselves. It is our body's way of drawing attention to what we are thinking and feeling.

Most of us do not breathe properly and use only a small part of our lungs; this is often due to factors such as illness, stress and poor lifestyle issues, such as bad posture and lack of exercise. We can change the bad habit of inefficient breathing by short, but regular, sessions of conscious breathing.

The breathing process

The process of breathing begins with the movement of the diaphragm, the large muscle at the base of the ribcage that forms the floor of the chest. Each breath is initiated by a signal from the respiratory centre of the brain to flatten the diaphragm downwards. The cavity enclosed by the ribcage is enlarged, thus creating a vacuum effect in the space. The lungs are suspended in this cavity and immediately expand to fill the space, drawing in air via the nose or mouth. The diaphragm then relaxes upwards, which deflates the lungs, forcing the breath to be expelled.

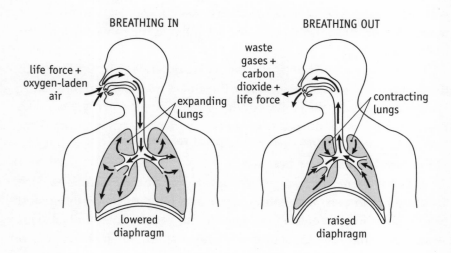

Figure 1: The breathing process

When we breathe normally, we inhale air through the nose. The nose is divided into two narrow cavities by a partition, the septum, which is made of bone and cartilage. The nostrils are lined with fine hairs that can filter out dust and other foreign particles from the air. If too many particles accumulate, the sneezing spasm is triggered. The mucous membrane in the nasal cavity moistens and warms the air as it is breathed in. The air then passes over the back of the mouth, down past the larynx (voice box), into the trachea (windpipe), where it then branches into the left and right bronchial tubes (bronchi) and further into the left and right lungs (see Figure 2). The lungs are like bags that are lined with a fine membrane containing millions of air sacs (the alveoli), which contain blood vessels with walls so thin that oxygen and carbon dioxide can easily pass into and out of the blood. It's amazing to think that if the lungs with all their alveoli were completely flattened out, they would cover an area of about 75 square metres.

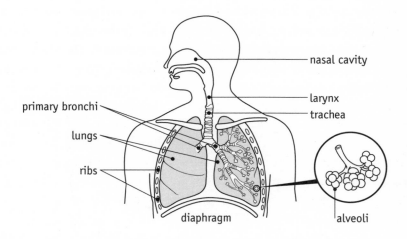

Figure 2: The organs of respiration

Essentially, there are two breaths: the in-breath and the out-breath, inhalation and exhalation, which you feel as different sensations. As air is taken into the lungs, oxygen passes through their fine membranes and into the bloodstream to oxygenate the cells and tissues of all the organs in the body, especially the brain. Every cell in the body needs oxygen to carry out its functions and to release energy from its chemical activities. As you exhale, waste gases, such as carbon dioxide, from body processes are conveyed to the lungs. Via the fine membranes of the lungs, waste products can be expelled from the bloodstream and released with the out-breath. All this happens in a few seconds, creating one of the body's great rhythmic movements.

There is a footnote to this basic process. Breathing is not something happening to you alone. Life finds good use for what we may consider to be waste products. The whole plant world takes in carbon dioxide from the air and, through its life processes, expels oxygen, which is then available to animal life. This is the beautiful picture of our inter-dependence. The next time you breathe consciously, consider where the oxygen you so vitally need might have come from and where the carbon dioxide you are giving away might be going.

Nasal breathing versus mouth breathing

Breathing through the nose is the ideal way to breathe because there are health benefits from allowing air to travel into the lungs via the nose and the delicately thin bones of the skull, or the sinuses. By entering our bodies through this route, the air is warmed, making oxygen more available to the fine membranes that line the inside of the lungs. Air is filtered by the nasal passages and the sinuses, and this filtering process creates pressure in the lungs during exhalation, which allows the lungs more time to extract oxygen into the blood. This helps maintain the body's equilibrium of oxygen and carbon dioxide, which ensures the pH or acidity balance of the blood. Because the nasal passages and sinuses moisten the air we take in, nasal breathing also helps prevent dehydration, and conditions such as laryngitis, which occur when the throat is dry.

A healthy person normally breathes through the nose. During vigorous exercise, we inhale through the open mouth as well as the nose, in order to supply sufficient oxygen to the muscles. But air entering via the mouth is not warmed or filtered, and the mouth soon dries out, and if carbon dioxide is expelled too quickly, which often happens in mouth breathing, oxygen absorption is actually decreased. Hence, any vigorous aerobic exercise can leave us gasping. For this reason, we should try to exercise with the mouth closed for as long as comfortably possible. When there is a need to open the mouth during exercise, the ideal would be to take breaks to do some closed-mouth, or nasal, breathing.

The gasp reflex

There are many occasions when we find ourselves literally gasping for air. If you have ever been suddenly immersed in cold water, whether this was intended or not, you have experienced the sudden contraction in the bronchial tubes at the top of the lungs – the bronchospasm, or gasp reflex. This automatic reaction is designed to prevent water from entering our lungs, but it also prevents air from entering, too. We can run out of air for a variety of reasons and almost always this leads to spasmodic breathing.

There are two brain-cell pathways that drive breathing and keep the brain in touch with every aspect of breathing, including the movement of the diaphragm. In one pathway, the neurons, or nerve cells, in the brain communicate with one another via electrically charged sodium atoms; while in the other pathway, neurons communicate via electrically charged calcium atoms. If the body is short of air for any reason, both of these pathways shut down, so the body, unable to receive any other respiratory messages from the brain, focuses its energy on gasping. Similarly, if one pathway becomes blocked, the other compensates, causing us to gasp. By gasping, oxygen supplies are restored and the heart is jolted back into action so that normal breathing can resume as quickly as possible. This is the powerful mechanism that can enable resuscitation when breathing has stopped.

It is worth pausing for a moment to reflect on the different ways in which your body looks after you, in terms of breathing and the breath. Breath connects us to air, to all the air around us, to everyone who is breathing air, to all other beings who, like us, depend on air. When we take this on board, we have to think twice about polluting the air.

Full-breath breathing

When the poet Sylvia Plath contemplated her sleeping son, she described his breath as 'soft as a moth'. How different is this to the way you generally breathe? Full-breath breathing is also known as 'soft-belly breathing' because it encourages the relaxation of the abdomen and discourages the tense, hard-belly approach to body posture. The soft-belly posture allows you to breathe deeply and gently so that you are calm and balanced, with your centre of gravity below your navel.

The breath of life is so much more than our unconscious breathing in and out. The in-breath is a way of taking in and receiving what we need, and the out-breath allows energy to escape and for us to give back to the part of life that nourishes us. Furthermore, anything that needs to escape, to be released, or to find a way out of the system, can do so with the out-breath. When you use the breath in this way, to let go of stress or anxiety for example, it is helpful to do so with an open mouth, since this reminds you that your conscious out-breath has this function.

As babies, we all know how to breathe most appropriately and efficiently, but the pressures and stresses of life tend to inhibit our natural instinct so that, in some cases, the loss of this skill can happen in early childhood. You can recover the skill of effective breathing with the exercise that follows. This is full-breath breathing. Full-breath breathing will introduce you to the benefits of breathing deeply and effectively.

EXERCISE 2

Full-breath breathing – the ideal

This is the key exercise in the book and the foundation for most of the exercises that follow. Once you have fully understood it and can practise it at will, it will become your Breath of Unity and the basic breath of self-healing.

Full-breath breathing allows your abdomen, as well as your chest, to fully expand when you inhale and to contract inwards as you exhale. All the muscles of respiration are involved. This way of breathing opens your awareness to your moment-by-moment unity with the Source and re-educates your physical body about

exercise continues ▶

efficient energy breathing, and thus maximises your ability to take in available energies and to expel what is no longer required.

Full-breath breathing rebalances the whole system, realigns all aspects of your being and encourages the flow of healing energies. It is an essential self-healing activity to improve breathing capacity and rhythm and benefit your entire physical system.

- Sit comfortably in a chair, with your feet flat on the ground and your back straight. If necessary, lift your head until you can feel it aligned with your back. Let your hands rest comfortably on your thighs or in your lap.

- Be aware of your breathing. Allow it to become slow, deep and gentle.

- Notice what your chest and abdomen are doing. As you breathe in your normal, habitual way, which part of your body is moving the most?

- In full-breath breathing, the focus is on the movement of the abdomen, rather than the chest. Put your hands on your abdomen and imagine it is a balloon you are going to fill with your breath and then empty.

- As you slowly inhale through the nose, allow your 'balloon' to fill by letting your abdomen gently expand, without straining.

- Exhale slowly and feel the balloon of your abdomen deflate, without straining.

- Practise this exercise two more times, noting the difference between the in-breath and the out-breath, and how you feel as you breathe like this.

After several weeks of practising full-breath breathing, and of raising your awareness through repeated remembrance of the sacred nature of the breath, you should find that you have an increased facility within your body to receive and give life energy through the breath.

The back, your health, posture and efficient breathing

The integrated set of spinal vertebrae carries the skull, the two girdles of the shoulders and pelvis, and the ribcage which encloses the lungs, heart and liver. The total vertebral column provides a protective tube for the spinal cord leading from the brain, allowing the neural network to penetrate every part of the body. At a subtle level, the physical corridor of the spine also facilitates the flow of vital subtle energy.

Thus, your back is a crucial feature of both your physical and subtle being. Optimum health must include looking after your back, and this means understanding its place in breathing and how efficient breathing strengthens the back and keeps it flexible. Many people suffer from some kind of back problem and the most common is lower back pain. People with this problem often wear an elastic corset to provide external support for the lumbar region of the spine. This 'corset' actually exists within our own bodies in the form of the abdominal muscles – the transverse abdominals at a deep level, combined with the upper layer of the internal oblique muscles. These two sets of muscles together make up a physical girdle extending from the ribcage to the lower abdomen.

The role of the abdominal muscular girdle

During breathing, the transverse abdominal muscles draw in the abdominal wall and work with the diaphragm to assist its movement. The muscle fibres run horizontally around the trunk, attached at the bottom of the ribcage and the tops of the hips. As the muscle contracts, pulling inward, it compresses and supports the abdominal organs. This provides important support for the trunk, holding the ribcage and pelvis in correct alignment with each other. The fibres of the upper internal oblique muscles run in diagonal directions and provide a complementary second layer of support. During breathing, they work in tandem with the transverse abdominals and provide primary support for the trunk.

The two sets of muscles expand outwards when we inhale and contract inwards as we exhale. Full-breath breathing actively stretches the abdominal muscles, using both lengthening and shortening movements. The abdominal muscles are effectively retrained to move outwards on inhalation and to pull inwards during exhalation.

In the next exercise, full-breath breathing is combined with conscious control of the abdominal muscle girdle during exhalation to strengthen your body's own natural 'corset'.

EXERCISE 3

Breathing to support your back

This exercise is carried out lying on your back, although it can be done sitting in a chair when lying down is not practicable.

- Lie down on a firm surface with your legs almost together. Move your arms about a foot away from your body with your palms facing upwards. If you have lower back pain, put a pillow or rolled towel under your knees to relieve pressure on the lower back.

- Take three full breaths into your abdomen, inhaling through your nose if possible. Allow your body to relax. Consciously breathing through the nose helps induce the body's relaxation response. As you exhale, notice how your abdomen moves inwards.

- Now gently lengthen and slow down your breathing rhythm as you breathe comfortably through your nose. As you exhale, consciously, but slowly, pull in your abdomen. Allow your body to find its own rhythm as this new activity is introduced.

- Continue for six more breaths.

- Lie quietly with your eyes closed for at least 3–5 minutes. Pay attention to any sensations in your body and any emotions or thoughts which might arise. Later, you could make a note of your reactions to, and progress with, the exercise in your healing journal.

exercise continues ▶

To strengthen your back, or if you suffer from lower back pain, you can practise this exercise once a day until any discomfort begins to ease. However, always consult a medical practitioner first if you have any kind of back problem.

Discovering the power of conscious breathing

The next exercise extends the technique of conscious full-breath breathing in order to encourage a steady rhythm to the breathing cycle. Further, practising this exercise can help you, or someone with whom you may be working, realise that it is possible to gain this level of control over your breath quite simply. Therefore this exercise can also be used to remind yourself that, through conscious breathing, you can find empowerment in other areas of your life.

EXERCISE 4
The rise and fall of the breath

Here, the breath is used to regulate your life rhythm and to help you become aware of this life rhythm. The exercise may also be used for self-healing. It may be carried out on its own or after any of the previous exercises.

- After a short session of full-breath breathing, continue to sit comfortably in a chair with your feet flat on the ground, breathing normally.

- As you breathe, notice the expansion and contraction, the rise and fall, of your belly. As you inhale and exhale, relax into your own rhythm of the rising and falling.

- Think of the rise and fall of your belly as the rhythm of your breath, which parallels the rise and fall of your life experi-

exercise continues ▶

ences. Just as you can witness the rise and fall of your belly during breathing, so you can also witness the ups and downs of your life in the same way.

- The ups and downs of your life are the experiences of your personality, but you do not have to define yourself by these experiences. Sit with this thought and let it 'breathe' into your consciousness.

- You do not have to define yourself in terms of success or failure. Sit with this thought and let it 'breathe' into your consciousness.

- It is time to honour your experiences. They are all part of your life journey. Sit with this thought and let it, too, 'breathe' into your consciousness.

- The rise and fall of your belly complement each other as part of a complete whole. In the same way, the ups and downs of your life complement each other as part of a complete whole. You are the silent, compassionate witness. Congratulate your-self on arriving at this place of understanding.

How have you reacted to each stage of the exercise? Note these feelings in your healing journal.

As you will have discovered during the previous exercise, because the life force is directly linked to the Source, this subtle component of the breath gives breathing exercises an important self-healing dimension: the power to reorganise and readjust our minds, attitudes and perspectives about life. Before you move on to the next chapter, take some time to recall moments in your life when you were made aware of your breathing. This includes losing as well as gaining control of your breathing. Your recollections and reflections could be entered in your healing journal.

Chapter 3

Breathing and subtle energies

The subtle role of breathing

In 1807, the poet William Wordsworth recalled the magic of his early childhood as a time

> When meadow, grove, and stream,
> The earth and every common sight,
> To me did seem
> Apparelled in celestial light,
> The glory and the freshness of a dream.

Many are able to recall similar childhood experiences and, for some, these experiences continue into adult life. Wordsworth's 'celestial light' refers to the ability of many young children to perceive the emanation of subtle energy from both the natural world and the human person as a light around their forms. This chapter looks in more detail at the cause of these emanations and how subtle energies play a central role in breathing.

A body of light

The Earth is a unique destination for the journeying soul, and it is important to honour our home planet as well as the fact that we are all equal manifestations of the Source. Each of us, when we come to

Earth, embarks on a life adventure that will be unique to us. We do not know where anyone else is on their soul journey. We do not always know why people or situations present themselves as they do. What we do know is that, along with the Earth and the whole natural world, we are journeying together. For these reasons, our love for ourselves, each other, and the world around us should always be unconditional.

From a healing point of view, the soul, or higher self, exists *before* physical life and after physical death too. But for a soul to physically incarnate and engage in the total experience of physicality, it needs the much denser energy form of the physical body. Before the physical body can be formed, the soul first creates the subtle structures that will support and make possible our physical body. The subtle structures, which we describe later in this chapter, may be imagined as a body of light, or as a body of subtle energy.

Once our physical body is established, we begin to develop an individual personality and consciousness from the time of conception onward. As we have all experienced, the problem with our conscious personality is that it càn easily convince us that *it* is the real us. Only pressure from our higher self, our soul, encourages us to consider that we have a far greater consciousness. When the personality becomes unconscious, as it does during sleep and at death, the higher self withdraws from the physical body, allowing us to move into a more subtle level of consciousness.

To be conscious of our physical state, we also have the mental abilities of mind: the capability to create thought; intelligence, which determines the level and quality of thought; and will, the power to drive thought into action. Mental energies travel at a far greater speed than light, and they vibrate at a far greater frequency than the energies of the physical body. Therefore, mental energies are able to project beyond the physical body. This mental energy 'body' is invisible to normal sight but is detectable by our subtle, intuitive senses. All thoughts, all actions, interactions and reactions, are processed in this mental 'body'.

When our positive or negative thoughts interact with physical life, emotions are generated as energies. These emotional energies, though not vibrating as fast as thought, still vibrate at a far greater rate than the physical body and so, again, project beyond it, creating another energy 'body'. In this subtle energy body, our emotions and emotional reactions are processed. Feelings generated by the higher self, acting as signals of warning, confirmation, or guidance, are also processed in this emotional part of our being.

In short, our spiritual, mental and emotional levels, or 'bodies', all vibrate at speeds greater than the speed of light. Thus, their energies are *subtle*, and they can be detected through the subtle senses. We all have a natural ability to use our subtle senses, which are actually essential to our survival. As you develop a new awareness and a new consciousness about the breath and breathing, you will be able to reactivate this ability.

The etheric level

There are vast differences between the vibratory frequencies of the physical body and the frequencies of our spiritual, mental and emotional energy bodies. To facilitate the flow of subtle energies to and from every level of our being, there is an energetic bridging level known as the *etheric* level. This allows energy to be stepped down in frequency as it moves towards the physical, and stepped up as it moves in the other direction. The etheric bridging level, vibrating slightly faster than the frequency of the physical body, effectively creates another energy body around it.

We owe the discovery of the etheric part of our being to the seers, or clairvoyants, of the ancient world who identified this luminous layer that radiates from all human beings. In some parts of the ancient world, this etheric substance was considered to be a fifth element, sitting alongside the four classical elements of Earth, Fire, Water and Air. Many Greek thinkers, for example, considered that the four elements alone did not account for their own observations of life and matter. In the fourth century BCE, Aristotle argued that life also included a 'heavenly' indestructible fifth element, which he termed *ether*. Later, the Roman Catholic Church endorsed Aristotle's concept of ether, supporting the view of earthly life as impermanent and heaven as eternal.

In India, the fifth element was termed *akasha*, and was regarded as an energetic luminous substance, from which all life is formed. According to ancient Indian spirituality, Brahman (the Creator, the

Source) used akasha to create the other four elements, and all human experience is contained with the akashic records. Hinduism thus describes akasha in terms that very much tally with the findings of modern clairvoyants and healers: it is the subtle substance of the etheric level, ether.

Your energy field

Our total energy pattern is thus a series of energy bodies surrounding the physical body. As their vibratory frequency increases, the sequence ranges from the etheric body, through the emotional and mental bodies, to the soul, or higher self (see Figure 3). But we are not bodies within bodies, like a set of Russian dolls. The important distinction is that the different rates of vibration between the energetic levels allow them to be *interpenetrating* rather than simply fitting one inside the other. Thus, whatever is happening energetically at one level will have an effect on all the other levels of our being. For example, when we mentally perceive a threat to our survival, we also sense the threat as an emotion such as fear, and this activates the necessary survival hormones, such as adrenaline, in the physical body. All the time the higher self acts as an observer (or overseer) of all of these energetic activities.

In other words, all these aspects – physical, etheric, emotional and mental – are one, aspects of the whole, higher self. Each 'body' radiates specific energies, creating a total field around you, known to the ancient Greeks as the *avra* (aura). The aura appears as a glowing emanation that some people sense as different moving colours, while others may sense the field as sound, feelings, or indescribable sensations. The aura, or energy field, is the 'celestial light' that Wordsworth saw as a child.

The human energy field contains evidence of the soul's experiences in its embodied form on Earth. Intuitive and clairvoyant vision is able to detect this material. We can be aware of the vibrations in our own field and we can also be aware of the energy fields of others, those of animals, plants and minerals, and the universal field which surrounds us. Many people are born with this awareness close to the surface.

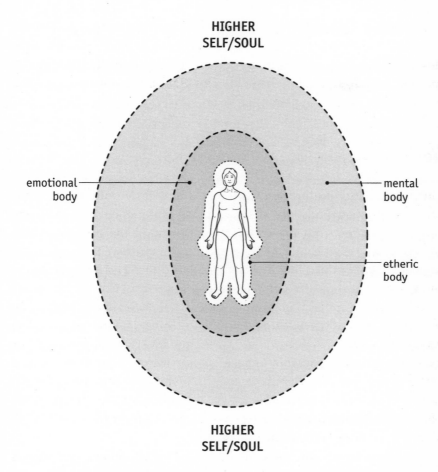

Figure 3: Your energy field. Your whole field is involved
in the breathing process

When different energy fields meet

When we encounter another person, we tend to decide very quickly
if we like them or not. At a subtle level, we immediately sense the
person's energy field, which gives us instant information about them.
How our energies relate to those of another person is the basis of
compatibility. Of course our mind can, and often does, override our
intuition or subtle sensing. Perhaps the subtle information is negative,
yet the person actually *looks* nice to us. We can choose whether to
listen to the message from our intuition or the one from our mind.

The etheric body

The etheric body can be seen as a misty layer of light, projecting four or five centimetres beyond the physical body, which is most often apparent to normal vision when a person is standing against a white or pale background. The etheric body extends beyond the physical body because its energies are vibrating at a slightly higher frequency. The etheric body has a shape somewhat like the human form, with an outer surface composed of a glowing web-like structure, the whole appearing to be illuminated from within.

The luminous depths of the etheric body are seen to contain hundreds of even brighter lines of light. These are the transparent channels that convey the flow of subtle energies. Where the channels intersect, a node or vortex of light is formed. This gives the etheric body the appearance of a starry sky at night.

The nodes of light are the subtle energy centres of the etheric body (these are also known as *chakras*); the more channels that converge, the larger the energy centre. All the centres are engaged in some aspect of processing and monitoring of energy flow.

The subtle energy centres

The etheric body has some 360 chakras or subtle energy centres, varying in size and function. Seven larger centres are seen to be connected to a central channel aligned with the spine. Their function is to allow the flow of energy to and from the various levels of our being and to process the energies generated by specific life issues, such as survival, sexuality and love. To fully understand the effects and purpose of the breathing exercises in this book, you need to have a working knowledge of the seven main energy centres. They act as the gateways, and gatekeepers, of our life journey, our health and our well-being. For these reasons, do not attempt to shut off their activity by 'closing' them. Although specific processes are going on in each centre, the energetic system operates as a complete and interconnected whole. Through etheric consciousness, each centre is aware of all the others' activities in the system.

The main centres appear as slight depressions in the luminous web-like surface of the etheric body. Each is attached to the central channel, aligned with the spine, which is in turn connected to the network of channels running through the etheric body. When a centre is activated, the vortex of light moves out from the surface of the etheric body to project into the energy field. It now appears as a bell- or funnel-shaped structure connected at its narrower end to the central channel. This shape facilitates the gathering in or radiating out of energies. I will refer to the seven main centres as the 'energy centres'.

The seven life gateways of the main energy centres

The subtle energy system and its seven energy centres regulate the intake and release of subtle energy. The system works with the breath and breathing to access these subtle energies. A disturbance in any of the subtle bodies, whether mental, emotional, or etheric, reveals itself in poor or interrupted breathing. Similarly, poor or disturbed breathing has an effect on the subtle bodies, via the system of energy centres. This highlights the relationship between the role of our breathing, our past and present life experiences, and the life issues that each centre processes. With this in mind, we will take a brief look at the position of the centres in your body and the life issues that each of your energy centres is processing.

Though rooted in the etheric body, the seven main centres may be detected in the positions mentioned below, in line with the physical spine (see Figure 4, overleaf). The spine, therefore, not only has the roles of mechanical support and protection, it also acts as the corridor for subtle energy as it moves into the physical body and the physical environment. In discussing the energy centres we will move in the same direction as the flow of their energies – from the base to the crown. Remember, the centres are *etheric*, or subtle energetic structures.

- The **base centre** is located at the base of the spine. This centre processes all issues of a physical nature: how we relate to our body and its physicality, our senses, sensuality, our sex or gender (and keep in mind there are two polarities, male and female, within each of us), our safety and survival, self-defence and aggression, our

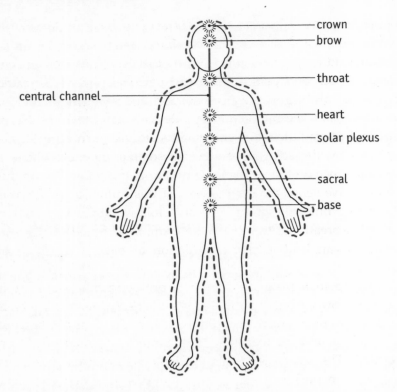

Figure 4: The position of the seven main energy centres
of the etheric body

relationship to all aspects of the natural world, and our relationship
to the planet. These issues are all related to our basic human nature.
The base centre is the keeper of cellular memory for the whole body.
When in a state of balance, the base centre vibrates to the colour red.

*(All centre colours may be seen with subtle vision and are similar, but
not identical, to the colours of the rainbow.)*

- The **sacral centre** is located opposite the sacral bones in the spine,
  between the navel and the base centre. The sacral centre processes
  all issues of creativity and sexuality. All creations have their be-
  ginnings and gestation here. The sacral centre has a special link
  with the throat centre, where the life issues that the sacral centre
  processes are given expression. When in a state of balance, the
  sacral centre vibrates to the colour orange.

- The **solar plexus centre** is located above the navel, just below the breastbone and the diaphragm. The processing of our thoughts, emotions and feelings is carried out by this centre, as well as generating our sense of personal self and personal power. The mind alerts us to problems, even when these are imagined or of our own making. So the mind can generate feelings of fear and alarm that can, in turn, affect our emotional state. All such energies are processed by the solar plexus centre so that they then have a direct influence on the movement of the diaphragm and so on our breathing. We sense the early stages of this influence as nervous feelings like 'butterflies in the stomach', followed by interrupted or constricted breathing. In its extreme form, interrupted diaphragm movement can lead to hyperventilation or even a cessation of breathing.

  Thus, the solar plexus centre has a profound influence on our breathing, how we breathe and our attitude to the breath. Additionally, through the interactions of this centre we discover much about our emotions and the workings of our mind, and their effects on breathing. The solar plexus centre demonstrates how conscious breathing can positively change these effects. It is here that conscious breathing reveals clues to personal empowerment.

  In its balanced state, the solar plexus centre vibrates to the colour golden yellow.

- Located in the centre of the chest (but not in the physical heart), the **heart centre** is considered to be the place of the soul. It is also the energy centre that governs both the breathing process and the flow of healing energies. This makes the heart centre crucial to breathing and all healing. The challenge of the heart centre is to express the light of the soul as love, to get its soul message of love through to us and to deal with all issues about love, and lovelessness, in our life.

  When in a state of balance it vibrates to the colour green, the colour of balance. It is not surprising that, when we need to revive and refresh ourselves, we often go somewhere in nature, unconsciously seeking the energies of the colour green. Many of the breathing exercises, with their simple ways to bring balance and healing, are a positive response to the challenge from the heart centre to make our life love-based, rather than fear-based.

- Though located in the throat and affecting its related organs, the **throat centre** is the 'ear, nose and throat' centre too. It links with the body and these organs via the thyroid gland. The throat centre is the third important centre to have a direct influence on our breathing. The throat centre has an important energetic link with the sacral centre, where everything creative is conceived and gestated. The centre processes all issues of expression and communi-cation, and all the different methods we use to express ourselves and communicate with others, with the world, as well as with the realms of the sacred. When in a state of balance, the throat centre vibrates to the colour sky-blue. This is often the colour of healing energies as perceived by subtle sensing.

  If you find yourself suffering from discomfort in the throat, this can be relieved by visualising that you are breathing a sky-blue-coloured light into the throat. Do this slowly and gently with six breaths, letting go of the pain, and thoughts and feelings about the issue, with the out-breath.

- The **brow centre** is located in the middle of the forehead, just above the brow. One of the roles of the brow centre is to oversee the operation of the energy centres below it. When subtle energies arrive here for transmission to the crown, the brow will send them back down the system if they have not been properly processed – i.e., if we have not dealt with the relevant issues.

  The brow centre processes information from our psychic awareness, or subtle sensing (our so-called sixth sense) as well as information from our intuitive awareness, or soul sensing. Both forms of energetic information are passed to the solar plexus centre, via its special link with the brow. Here, energetic information meets with the mind which then attempts to understand it.

  When we breathe, the life force in the breath is instantly recognised by the brow centre. The brow monitors the quality of the life force entering and exiting our subtle and physical bodies. When balanced, the brow centre vibrates to a deep royal blue or indigo colour.

- The **crown centre** is located at the crown of the head. The centre is our link with the Source and deals with issues of our spirituality. The crown centre links with the body via the pineal gland located in the centre of the brain, which tells us about the amount of sunlight we are getting and whether we are getting enough. This gland also mirrors the crown centre's role of telling us about the amount of spiritual light we are allowing into our life and whether this is enough.

When we do not get enough sunlight, as those who live in grey climates well know, we feel depressed. If deprivation goes on long enough, this can develop into the medical condition known as seasonal affective disorder (SAD syndrome). The remedy is to get some sunlight as soon as possible or practise an appropriate breathing exercise, such as Exercise 54: Walking and breathing in the Sun (see page 180). When in a state of balance, the crown centre vibrates to the colour violet.

The template for the physical body

The template for the formation, development and composition of the physical body is found in the etheric body. Thus, the symmetry of the physical body is derived from the symmetry of the etheric body, with its central channel and network of energy centres; the body's ability to process the flow of substances to and from its organs is derived from the flow of energies in the etheric channels; and the seven main energy centres are the structures from which the seven endocrine glands (the pineal, pituitary, thyroid, thymus, Islets of Langerhans in the pancreas, ovaries or testes and adrenal glands) are derived.

Other physical organs originate in other large energy centres. The nervous system is derived from the etheric energy channels while the vascular, or blood system derives from the flow of energies within the etheric network. The fact that we can absorb subtle energies through the skin is due to the presence of tiny energy centres throughout the surface of the etheric body. These foundations of the physical body have a direct bearing on how and whether healing and other beneficial energies flow into the body from a spiritual level.

The etheric level and the subtle energies of the breath

Via our breathing, the etheric level conveys the life force, essential to the animation of all physical forms, to the relevant energy centres for processing. The etheric level also conveys vitalising energies, entering via the sacral and solar plexus energy centres, to the body tissues. In this way, the etheric level is the energetic support system for physical life. This bridging level, between the physical and the non-physical, is the entry point where the higher self and its subtle energies can take physical form.

The etheric level acts as the communication vehicle for the higher self, or soul, enabling the passage of energies from the higher self to the physical and from the physical back to the higher self. In doing so, the energy centres act as a distribution system for all the energies, including the mental and emotional energies, generated during life experience. Throughout these activities, the centres identify subtle energies and, if possible, process them. But very often a person is not ready to deal with a certain situation, or trauma. In that case, the etheric consciousness stores the relevant energies for processing later.

However, if unprocessed material is allowed to build up, we begin to receive warning signals from the higher self, in the form of uncomfortable feelings. If these are not heeded, the body may become sick so that we are forced to listen to these warnings. Similarly, whenever a person confronts a situation contrary to the personal spiritual core, the energy centres work hard to process the material. But continued exposure makes this progressively more difficult, which can exhaust the centres and lead to energetic blockage and subsequent ill-health. To give a simple and common example: a person experiences the loss of a loved one and soon develops a severe cold. This is because the immune system, via the thymus gland in the centre of the chest, is linked to the heart centre, which deals with all issues concerning love. The feelings of grief have manifested as a shock to the immune system, leaving the person vulnerable to infection.

Energetic hygiene and the Closing-down Procedure

Now that you are familiar with the location of your energy centres, at this point you need to remember that an essential part of your breath work is to look after yourself and your energy field. If you wish to follow a breathing exercise, or a session of exercises, with some other spiritual practice, such as meditation, you are in the ideal state to do this. If not, you should be aware that your efforts have opened your energy centres more than is needed for everyday functioning. In other words, you no longer need to be open to that level of energy flow and you need to 'close down' the advanced state of openness. This may be done by carrying out the Closing-down Procedure set out below.

The Closing-down Procedure realigns your energy centres and protects your energy field. This is particularly necessary if you are going to expose yourself to normal, everyday situations, such as the routine supermarket trip, where you would be too open to external energies. When your breathing session is in the evening, the Closing-down Procedure also ensures sound sleep. 'Closing down' means returning your subtle energy system to everyday functioning; it is linked to closing your practice sessions. It does not, however, mean fully closing the energy centres or shutting down any of the body systems.

EXERCISE 5

The Closing-down Procedure

This exercise is in three parts. The first part clears incompatible energies, using the clearing energy of silver light. The standing stance aligns the centres, facilitates grounding, and frees the energy circuits to flow appropriately.

Part A: Clearing your energy field

- If possible, stand with your feet shoulder-width apart and your arms hanging loosely by your sides. Gently flex the

exercise continues ▶

knees and allow your body to relax. Use the breath to aid with relaxation and attunement or centring.

- Take a moment to be aware of any heavy energy in your body and energy field, noting where it seems to have accumulated. (It is worth making a note of this observation in your healing journal every time you do this exercise to see if there is a pattern.)

- Now visualise yourself under a shower or gentle waterfall of silver light. Breathe in. As you exhale, let this light pour over you, through you, and out into your surrounding energy field, especially to any place where you sensed an accumulation of heavy energy. Allow the light to exit through your hands and feet and every body orifice.

- Notice the colour of the light that moves in to fill the space that you have cleared. Your awareness of this colour will confirm that the clearing is taking place. You might sense this in a number of ways. If you feel you are sensing nothing (it is your mind saying you can't), carry out this important exercise as if you can.

- Note the sensations of clearing and the sensations of being cleansed.

Next, bring your energy centres back to a level of everyday functioning from being wide open.

Part B: Regulating your energy centres

Since your energy centres have a three-dimensional structure, you may find it helpful to visualise them as flowers with petals that are able to close up, but not shut tightly. The second part of this exercise is carried out by visualising the 'flowers' of each centre gently closing up a little. Your intention is to bring them to everyday functioning. See the colours as light.

exercise continues ▶

- Still standing relaxed, with your knees gently flexed, focus your attention on your crown centre. Visualise the 'flower' of your crown centre having the colour violet. Breathe in. As you exhale, visualise the 'petals' of your crown centre 'flower' closing up a little.

- Move your awareness to the brow centre, colour indigo or royal blue. Breathe in. As you exhale, visualise the centre's 'petals' closing up a little.

- Move your awareness to the throat centre, colour sky-blue. Breathe in. As you exhale, visualise the centre's 'petals' closing up a little.

- Move your awareness to the heart centre, colour green. Breathe in. As you exhale, visualise the centre's 'petals' closing up a little.

- Move your awareness to the solar plexus centre, colour golden yellow. Breathe in. As you exhale, visualise the centre's 'petals' closing up a little.

- Move your awareness to the sacral centre, colour orange. Breathe in. As you exhale, visualise the centre's 'petals' closing up a little.

- Move your awareness to the base centre, colour glowing red. Breathe in. As you exhale, visualise the centre's 'petals' closing up a little.

- Now notice the first colour that comes to mind. This is the colour of energy that will keep your system in place. Breathe in and, as you exhale, surround yourself with a sphere of this coloured light.

This is also a grounding process. Note the direction of activity: from the highest vibration of the crown centre to that closest to the Earth at the base centre.

exercise continues ▶

Follow with the final third part of the Closing-down Procedure. This will keep your energy field strong and protect you by not allowing entry of incompatible energies.

Part C: The Sphere of Protection

• Still standing relaxed and breathing naturally, visualise golden light. Breathe in and, as you exhale, surround the sphere of coloured light with a sphere of golden light. See this golden sphere sparkle and gleam. This will tell you about its energy of strength and protection. Spend a moment of awareness there before moving back into your everyday consciousness.

Once you have learnt them, the three parts of the Closing-down Procedure should be practised as one complete exercise.

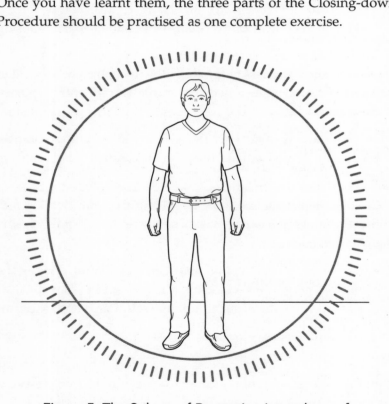

Figure 5: The Sphere of Protection is a sphere of golden light

The breathing energy field

As a person breathes, their aura, or energy field, breathes too. First, all the subtle energy centres pulsate in time to our breathing rhythm, and then their pulsations move out into the energy field. As we breathe, our aura expands on the in-breath and contracts on the out-breath.

Stress and trauma affect our breathing, and the effect of stress can also be seen by the movements of our energy field. During such times of disturbed breathing we take in less life force, and the activity of our energy centres is reduced. This is why so many of the exercises in the book involve the energy centres, and why they are the focus of attention for many subtle-energy healers.

The human rainbow

At a subtle level, we are walking rainbows. All the primary colours are needed to make a rainbow, and the fact that our energy centres vibrate to the colours of the rainbow tells us that our life is, and always was, a complete whole. There is no issue or experience that does not have a valid place in our unique story. With this in mind, it is helpful to recall the functions of the seven main energy centres in relation to our total being.

The lower three energy centres – the base, sacral and solar plexus – via the mind, exert a pressure on our personality to engage in humanness. Consequently, the personality may well, and often does, interpret its view of human life as all there is. The mind then tells us that there are plenty of logical and scientific arguments to support this view. The upper three centres of the crown, brow and throat, via our intuition and feelings, exert a pressure on the personality to recall our light, or spiritual, origins.

The heart centre shows us that we will only ever be half of what we can be until we take a leap of faith and trust in our reality as soul. Through its processing of love issues, the heart centre shows us that love is the key to a harmonious balance of both the physical and spiritual aspects of our being. This is the ultimate message of all seven levels of consciousness, especially the heart.

At the physical level of the breath, all seven centres are involved in breathing to a greater or lesser degree. However, the most prominent of the breathing centres are the heart, solar plexus and throat centres, because these have a direct relation to the function of the relevant physical organs. In the next exercise, you can work with the breath, and the colours of the seven main energy centres, to totally rebalance your energy centres and your energy field.

EXERCISE 6

Breathing the light of the centres

This exercise celebrates and totally balances your energy field through balancing your subtle energy centres. Use the exercise whenever you feel the need for energetic balance, but practise it only once in any one day. Breathing is the key to energising ourselves, and our breathing is influenced by our posture. Where it is possible, an effective standing posture (where your feet are shoulder-width apart with your feet flat on the ground and your knees relaxed) has the same energising aims of a relaxed body and a mind with which you can pay attention while letting all thoughts pass through unobstructed. The standing stance described opens up your energy field and allows energy to flow freely.

- Stand, or sit if necessary, with your feet shoulder-width apart. Let your arms hang loosely by your sides. As you straighten your back, relax your pelvis and shoulders. Let your centre of gravity move to the region of your sacral centre.

- Take a few breaths to clear your lungs. Allow any tension, worry, or anxiety to exit your body as you exhale through your open mouth. Close your mouth and breathe normally when you feel settled.

- You are going to fill your energy field with seven spheres of coloured light, from red to violet. These spheres of light are created by combining visualisation with the breath. You will visualise each sphere outside of the one you visualised before.

exercise continues ▶

- Breathe in, visualising red light rising from behind your heels, and moving up your back to the top of your head. Pause for a moment.

- As you exhale, visualise the red light moving down the front of your body until it is under your feet. You are now enclosed in a sphere of red light.

- Bring your attention back to your heels. Breathe orange light up your back to the top of your head, pause, and, on the out-breath, visualise the orange light moving down the front of your body until it is under your feet, totally enclosing the sphere of red light with a sphere of orange light.

- Returning your focus to your heels, this time breathe yellow light up your back to the top of your head, pause, and, on the out-breath, visualise the yellow light moving down the front of your body until it is under your feet. Enclose the sphere of orange light with a sphere of yellow light.

- Focus again on your heels, breathe green light up your back to the top of your head, pause, and, on the out-breath, visualise the green light moving down the front of your body until it is under your feet, totally enclosing the sphere of yellow light with a sphere of green light.

- Returning your focus to your heels, breathe sky-blue light up your back to the top of your head, pause, and, on the out-breath, visualise the blue light moving down the front of your body until it is under your feet. Enclose the sphere of green light with a sphere of sky-blue light.

- Focus on your heels once again and this time breathe royal blue/indigo light up your back to the top of your head, pause, and, on the out-breath, visualise the indigo light moving down the front of your body until it is under your feet, totally enclosing the sphere of sky-blue light with a sphere of indigo light.

exercise continues ▶

- Returning your focus to your heels for the final time, breathe violet/purple light up your back to the top of your head, pause, and, on the out-breath, visualise the violet light moving down the front of your body until it is under your feet, totally enclosing the sphere of indigo light with a sphere of violet light.

- With relaxed breathing, spend a few moments of awareness as you are totally enclosed in a rainbow of light.

The healthy functioning of our bodies depends on the work of the subtle energy centres. We also need a harmonious relationship with the flow of energies, into and out of the etheric body. Everything, all living things, both give out and receive energy. In the next chapter we will examine this energetic 'polarity'.

Chapter 4

Breathing and polarity

Subtle energies flow into and out of the etheric body, creating an energetic polarity. We are both receptive (we receive energy) and emissive (we give out energy). All living things, and the very workings of the Earth and the cosmos, depend on this energy cycle. It is part of the dual nature of the physical level, as reflected in the polar opposites of light and dark, hot and cold, and so on. Breathing and the breathing cycle underline this truth of being with every breath that we take.

The subtle aspects of polarity

On each side of the central channel of the etheric body, and connected to it, are two other channels that extend from the base to the brow centre (see Figure 6, overleaf). The circulation of energy in the two channels creates a balance between the inflow and outflow of energies throughout the subtle energy system. It is through these polarities being in balance that our dual identity as spiritual, as well as physical, beings is celebrated.

Historically, the energy polarities have been referred to as 'masculine' (emissive) and 'feminine' (receptive), based on the relative roles of male and female in procreation, but these polarity terms describe qualities of energy flow rather than aspects of gender. In this book they are referred to as the emissive and receptive energies.

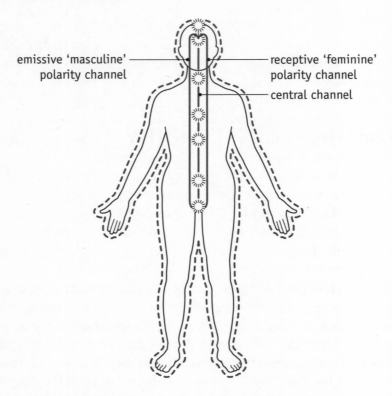

emissive 'masculine' polarity channel

receptive 'feminine' polarity channel

central channel

Figure 6: The polarity channels of the etheric body, present in all humans

Everyone has both channels and both energies. The emissive right side processes energies that are outgoing. The receptive left side processes energies that are incoming. The activities of the two energy channels create an energetic cycle. Both of these etheric polarity channels have a link with the brow centre at the etheric level, and the two nostrils at the physical level, further emphasising the importance of nasal breathing.

For emotional and mental health, as well as physical well-being, the energies of the two polarities should be in a state of balance; however, it is easy for them to get out of kilter. Our mental or emotional state, our thoughts or behaviour, have an instant effect on this balance. For example, when we are not assertive enough in a given situation, so that we allow ourselves to be disempowered, the emissive energies are not being mobilised when they need to be. The polarities are either thrown out of balance by the situation or their imbalance has caused us to be unable to stand up for ourselves. We then experience feelings such as anger, frustration, or self-disgust, which further serve as warning signals that our energies are out of balance. If this goes on for too long, so that one energy stream is unused or under-developed, the other will try to compensate by dominating the system and all its activities. This is self-defeating because it nurtures the initial weakness.

The cycle of breathing is derived from the dual aspects of the energy cycle: inhalation is the receptive part of the cycle, while exhalation is the emissive part. At a subtle level, these dual aspects of the energy cycle are processed via the two etheric polarity channels. Thus the life force has two complementary roles involving both aspects of the breathing and energy cycle. The sacred breath depends on polarity. Life itself depends on polarity and polarity is an expression of life.

Two sets of subtle energy centres help us to keep our links with planet Earth, with the 'heavens' and with the expression of love that joins these two sacred aspects of being. The two sole-of-the-foot centres and the two palm centres link the polarity of the planetary energies with the two etheric polarity channels. These may be accessed by visualising that the breath can enter and exit via the soles of the feet and the palms of the hands. (See Figure 7, overleaf.)

The energy centres of the hands

In Traditional Chinese Medicine and acupuncture, the *laogong* point on the palm of the hand is related to the heart, blood circulation and the release of negative *qi*, or heavy energy. This clue tells us about the vital energetic link between the centres of the two palms and the heart. The heart centre is the key to the subtle aspects of breathing and healing and the link means that the palms of each hand can act as extensions of the heart in conveying love and healing. Hence we may soothe, touch, caress and care for others with the hands. However, when the hands are used to hurt another there is a negative effect on the heart centre and our breathing rhythm. Try the next exercise to sense the hand–heart link.

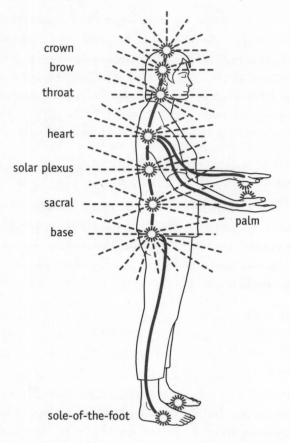

crown
brow
throat

heart

solar plexus

sacral

base

palm

sole-of-the-foot

Figure 7: The seven main energy centres and the energy centres of the hands and feet with the hand–heart and sole-of-the-foot–base links, showing projection of energies

EXERCISE 7

Sensing the hand–heart energy circuit

This exercise will extend the sensitivity you have discovered and activated through the exercises in the book so far. The first part focuses on drawing in energy, the second on giving it out.

exercise continues ▶

- Sit in a chair in a relaxed position with your legs uncrossed. Hold your palms out, facing away from you, with your arms bent at the elbow. Relax your elbows, the back of the neck, and the shoulders. Close your eyes if this helps your concentration. Breathe normally.

- Focus your attention on the palm centres. As you inhale, imagine that you are drawing energy in through the palm centres. Breathe out gently, focusing through the palms. Note your sensations.

- Now visualise the energetic link between your palms and your heart centre. Breathe in and sense energy moving up your arms, across your shoulders, to converge in the heart centre, in the middle of your chest.

- Lower your arms and relax for a few moments. Raise your arms again, with your hands held out in front of you as before. In this second part of the exercise you are going to send energy from the heart centre to the palms.

- Put your attention in the heart centre and relax. Breathe into the heart centre. As you exhale, visualise energy moving from the heart centre, out to the shoulders, down the arms, to the centre in each palm. What did you sense this time?

Compare your experiences of absorbing and transmitting energy via your breathing with the palm and heart centres, and make a note of the sensations in your healing journal.

The energy centres of the feet

Linked energetically with the base centre, the energy centres in the soles of the feet absorb energies from the Earth. These life-giving energies are essential to the physical body and physical life. This is why it is good to walk barefoot outside whenever you can, a practice that will lead to the pleasure of sensing the Earth in a deeper way. The soles of the feet act as grounding or earthing points, as does the base centre, for incoming subtle energies.

In Traditional Chinese Medicine and acupuncture, the *yongquan* point on the sole of the foot is connected to the kidneys and is a focus for treatment in cases of hypertension. This acupuncture point is in the same place as the sole-of-the-foot energy centre (just behind the middle of the two large pads at the front of the foot). Its function gives a clue to the link between the centres of the feet and the base centre, because base centre energies enter the body via the adrenal glands. These glands, situated at the top of the kidneys, secrete hormones associated with the need for 'fight or flight' and are thus involved in the bodily states of hypertension, stress or anxiety.

Let's see what you can sense with your sole-of-the-foot centres.

EXERCISE 8

Sensing Earth energies with the sole-of-the-foot centres

- Stand on the ground in a relaxed posture with bare feet shoulder-width apart. Take six slow full breaths. Breathe normally.

- Pay attention to the soles of your feet. Be aware of your contact with the Earth, as well as with the grass, soil, sand or whatever is under your feet. Close your eyes and notice whether you can sense an energetic flow via the soles of your feet.

- Still with your focus in the feet, use the in-breath to aid your awareness of the passage of energy from the ground into your feet, up your legs to the base centre. Inhale a few times with this intention.

Note your discoveries in your healing journal. Repeat the exercise in different locations and at different times of the day. What did you discover?

Your experiences with the two previous exercises should reinforce your understanding of the role of the hands and feet in absorbing subtle energy via conscious breathing. The sole centres, through their contact with the planet, keep us grounded by earthing energetic activity. Grounding ourselves is important for our efficient functioning as a channel for healing and other energies, and for channelling these to others. Through the palm centres we transmit subtle energies and absorb energetic information. During this activity, the centres enable us to perceive or sense the movement of subtle energies.

Therefore you can use your breath to keep in touch with the Earth, via your feet, and with your higher self, via your hands. These two sets of energy centres provide us with an opportunity to celebrate our love for the Earth (perhaps through dance and movement) and our love for others and the Earth family (perhaps through using the hands to heal, comfort, prepare food and make music).

Our hands and feet tell us much about polarity: how we communicate it, how it is part of our lives and how, in fact, polarity is another expression of Oneness. Every breath we take is a reminder of Oneness and the spiritual reality behind the polarity of the physical realm. We have ways of keeping in touch with the 'heavenly' realms, apart from via the crown centre, as the following breathing exercise shows.

EXERCISE 9

Opening to 'heavenly' energies

Our hands may hang at our sides for much of the time, but we can extend them in the opposite direction above our head. This stance is a natural expression of joy, bringing in positive feelings and combating depression.

- Stand on the ground in a relaxed posture with your feet shoulder-width apart. Take six slow full breaths. Breathe normally as you look up at the sky, and beyond.

- Put your attention down into the soles of your feet. Be aware of your contact with the Earth.

exercise continues ▶

- Raise your arms above you head, with your palms upwards.

- Visualise that you can breathe the energies of the Sun into your palm centres. Even if the Sun is not visible, you can still breathe in its energies. Enjoy the sensation of these energies circulating throughout your body. As you exhale, you are giving out the energies to the world.

- Visualise that you can breathe in the energies of the sky. Enjoy the sensation of these energies circulating throughout your body. As you exhale, you are giving out the energies to the world.

- Allowing your imagination to extend further, visualise that you can breathe in the energies of the cosmos. Enjoy the sensation of these energies circulating throughout your body. As you exhale, you are giving out the energies to All That Is.

Sun and Moon breathing

Life on Earth depends on the energy radiating out from the Sun. This energy is also received by the Moon before it is reflected towards us – a process evident during the darkness of the night sky. Wherever we are situated, we are aware of sunlight during the day and moonlight during the night. Life on Earth is bathed in this rhythm of light and the other unseen energies that accompany the light. Like the rhythm of our breathing, the cycle of light and energy is a primary rhythm of life. Life on Earth has evolved to align with the cycle of light so that each and every life form, whether plant or animal, lives to an individual rhythm. An aspect of evolution is that every individual rhythm is interdependent, creating a balanced whole. An example is the way most plants use the carbon dioxide exhaled by animals and give out oxygen as a by-product of their life processes. The oxygen given out by the plants is, in turn, used by animals.

As we breathe and interact with life, we are involved in creating, or possibly upsetting, this balanced whole. We sense when our personal rhythms are aligned with the natural rhythms outside us as a feeling of inner harmony. You have already discovered that your own inner harmony is reflected in your breathing. Thus, breathing is the short cut to recreating inner harmony. Inner harmony and the Breath of Unity are the same. Here we explore polarity through linking the personal rhythm of the breath and the emissive and receptive subtle energy streams with the natural rhythms generated by the Sun and Moon. In terms of energetic polarity, the Moon can represent the receptive ('feminine') energy stream and the Sun the emissive ('masculine') energy stream. The archetypal significance of the Sun and Moon has featured in the spiritual and religious life of humans from earliest times, both in terms of what they might represent and in terms of the liturgical or ceremonial calendar.

Lunar energies

The Moon travels round the Earth. Through its gravitational interaction with our planet, the Moon creates tidal movement within the oceans. It also creates energetic tides through its appearance in the night sky. All humans are affected by the Moon, but females are especially aware through their menstrual cycle of around twenty-nine days. This tidal cycle mirrors the lunar cycle of just over twenty-nine days – from the time of the waxing New Moon, through the Full Moon to its appearance of waning in the night sky. There are twelve to thirteen moons to each year of twelve months. Each moon exerts its own powerful energetic influence. As well as their physical influence, lunar energies also affect our emotions and the contents of the unconscious mind.

EXERCISE 10

Breathing lunar energies

This self-healing exercise draws your attention to the role of the Moon in your life and the life around you. Information on the Moon's phases can be found in the appropriate calendar for any

exercise continues ▶

month of the year. The exercise has two parts and has benefits that are relevant to both genders.

Part A

We can align with the energies of the New Moon to acknowledge or celebrate renewal, rebirth or the start of something new. Fulfilment is the mood of the Full Moon, while the waning Moon acknowledges decline, decay, and how the end of something leads to renewal and rebirth.

- If possible practise the exercise outdoors at night, although it is perfectly possible to remain indoors.

- Lie down on your back, stand or sit, in a relaxed posture facing the Moon or in moonlight.

- Breathe normally. Acknowledge the presence of the Moon in your life.

- Now take six full breaths. Your intention is to breathe in the energies of the Moon.

- As you exhale, imagine that the lunar energies spread throughout every level of your being.

- Rest and breathe normally. Acknowledge that you are at one with the Moon and its energies.

- You may wish to become more aware of those beings that have a nocturnal pattern of activity. Check that you are not getting cold!

- Before leaving your place, give thanks to the Moon for its gift to you and to life.

You may wish to extend this exercise by adding other relevant self-healing intentions.

exercise continues ▶

Part B

It is also possible to align ourselves, via the breath, with the energies of the Moon to enable any or all of the following:

To regularise the menstrual cycle

To balance the emotions

To reinforce the feminine polarity and expression of the feminine

To more fully express the receptive ('feminine') energy stream

To balance this stream with the emissive ('masculine') polarity within yourself

- For these purposes the exercise has its greatest effect just before, during and just after the Full Moon.

- Follow the same procedure as in Part A above and breathe six full breaths into your sacral centre – situated just below the navel.

- Rest and breathe normally. Acknowledge that you are at one with the Moon and its energies.

- Before leaving your place, give thanks to the Moon for its gift to you and to life.

Solar energies

Each new day is announced by the appearance of the Sun on the eastern horizon – sunrise or sun-up. The Sun is at its most powerful when it is most nearly overhead at around midday. The ending of each day is described by the going down of the Sun on the western horizon – sunset or sundown.

The passage of the Earth around the Sun takes a year. Because the angle of the Earth to the Sun changes as it moves, wherever we live, the least amount of sunlight and heat from the Sun occurs during winter. The Winter Solstice marks the time of the shortest day. The number of daylight and night-time hours is the same at the time of the two Equinoxes. The first Equinox that occurs after winter marks the first day of spring. The longest day is that of the Summer Solstice. The second Equinox marks the first day of autumn. All life is affected by the cycle of the Sun and its energies. The relevant points in the solar year may be found in an appropriate calendar. In the Northern Hemisphere, they tend to occur around 21/22 December (Winter Solstice), 21/22 March (Spring Equinox), 21/22 June (Summer Solstice) and 21/22 September (Autumn Equinox), with the seasons being reversed in the Southern Hemisphere.

EXERCISE 11

Breathing solar energies

This exercise focuses on the role of the Sun in your life and the life around you. It is in three parts and, in each case, take appropriate steps to protect yourself from too much exposure to the Sun's powerful rays.

Part A

We can align ourselves with the energies of the Sun every day at dawn to celebrate renewal, rebirth or the start of a new venture. Fulfilment is the mood of the midday Sun, while sunset is the time to acknowledge decline, decay, and to celebrate how endings often lead to renewal and rebirth.

- If possible practise this exercise outdoors, although you can do it indoors if you prefer.

- Lie down on your back, stand or sit, in a relaxed posture facing the Sun or in sunlight. Your eyes should be closed at all times during the exercise. Do not look directly at the Sun when it has moved to its brightest position in the sky.

- Breathe normally. Acknowledge the presence of the Sun in your life.

exercise continues ▶

- Now take six full breaths into the belly. Your intention is to breathe in the energies of the Sun. You may wish to focus on a specific situation with this intention.

- Exhale and imagine the solar energies spreading throughout every level of your being.

- Rest and breathe normally. You are at one with the Sun and its energies.

- Give thanks to the Sun for its gift to you and to life.

You may wish to extend this exercise by adding other relevant self-healing intentions.

Part B

It is also possible for us to align ourselves, via the breath, with the energies of the Sun to enable the following:

> To reinforce the masculine polarity within you and expression of the masculine

> To totally energise your whole system

> To more fully express the emissive ('masculine') energy stream

> To balance this stream with the receptive ('feminine') stream within yourself

- The exercise has its greatest effect just before, during and just after midday, with maximum benefits coming at the time of the Summer Solstice.

- Follow the same procedure as above and breathe six full breaths into your solar plexus centre – situated just below your ribcage and above your navel.

- Rest and breathe normally. Acknowledge that you are at one with the Sun; at one with its energies.

exercise continues ▶

- Become aware of those other living beings that are active at the time of your exercise.

- Before returning to your everyday activities, give thanks to the Sun for its gift to you and to life.

Part C

The annual progress of the Sun gives further self-healing opportunities for your personal journey through each year.

The time of the Winter Solstice is a time of moving into the 'dark', moving towards your *inner* light. This is the time to commune with your higher self and wait patiently for guidance from within.

The Spring Equinox is the time to experience the balance between the two tendencies of moving inward to the inner light of winter and moving outward to the outer light of summer. Where are you going and where have you been?

The Summer Solstice is a time of expressing who you really are (a spiritual being with a body), communing with the life of your personality and expressing what you discovered during your time with your inner light through your personality.

The Autumn Equinox is the time to experience the balance between the two tendencies of moving outward to the outer light of summer and moving inward to the inner light of winter. Again: where are you going and where have you been?

- For these purposes the exercise has its greatest effect just before, during and just after the day of the particular equinox or solstice.

- Follow the same procedure as at the beginning of the exercise and breathe six full breaths into your abdomen. As you exhale, allow the specific solar energies that you have chosen to work with to permeate your being on all levels.

- Rest and breathe normally. Acknowledge that you are at one with the Sun and its energies.

exercise continues ▶

- You may wish to become more aware of those beings (both plant and animal) that have a certain pattern of activity at the time you have chosen.

- Before leaving your place, give thanks to the Sun for its gift to you and to life.

Balance and polarity

Having gained insight into the balancing factors in your relationship with the Sun and Moon, you can look at the balance of your inner polarity with greater understanding. The symmetry of our bodies tells us about balance. As the Gospel of Thomas advises, balance is about 'making the two one'. We know that balance is essential to harmony, including the harmony of well-being. Optimal breathing is a balance of inhalation and exhalation and the pauses between these processes. At a subtle energetic level, optimal breathing also brings about a balance between the two energetic polarities of our body. We all experience the imbalance caused by emotional upset or the pressures of stress and we instinctively feel the need to return to a balanced state as soon as possible. The next exercise is designed to quickly achieve polarity balance in such situations. It is also an excellent exercise when you feel overwrought or panicky. Here, the Sun and Moon are symbolic of the two energetic polarities within you.

EXERCISE 12

The Balancing Breath

Known to many yoga practitioners as the Sun and Moon Breath, or Alternate Nostril Breathing, the effectiveness of this exercise is based on the fact that the two subtle polarity channels rise up

exercise continues ▶

on either side of the etheric body, converge, and end near the relevant nostril.

- Sit comfortably in a chair, with your legs and arms uncrossed. Make sure that your back and neck are straight with your head held erect but relaxed.

- Take three full breaths. Place the first two fingers of your right hand to the side of your right nostril and press gently to close it. Breathe in through the left nostril slowly and normally. Hold this breath for a count of three.

- Transfer the first two fingers of your right hand (or you can change to your left hand if you prefer) to the side of your left nostril to gently close it. Breathe out through the right nostril slowly and normally. Count to three.

- Breathe in through the right nostril. Hold this breath for a count of three. As you hold your breath, transfer your fingers to your right nostril, close it, and breathe out through your left nostril. This completes one breathing cycle.

Figure 8: The Balancing Breath

exercise continues ▶

- After completing the cycle slowly and gently, six times, sit quietly for a few moments. Let yourself become aware of the balance of energies in your body. Allow yourself to feel gratitude for this feeling of renewed health. The attitude of thankfulness after practising any exercise enhances its effects and sends a positive affirmation to the mind.

When our dual identity as spiritual and physical beings is disrupted, our higher self sends a message to our conscious self to remind us to do something about the situation. There are many factors in daily life that threaten our psychological and physical health, even our actual survival, and these threats trigger the soul message that we need to heal the situation. We interpret these threats as stress. In the next chapter, with balance in mind, we look at the role of breathing in helping us deal with stress.

Chapter 5

Breathing to counter stress

Stress has always been with us. It is our physiological and psychological response to events that threaten our personal balance in some way. These events may be real or simply what we perceive as threatening. For many of us, threats to loved ones may induce stress, too. When faced with such threats, whether they are to personal safety or to our mental or emotional equilibrium, our body initiates the biological stress response. This response is designed to protect and support us and it has been an effective response system for humans throughout time, from our ancestors who faced life-or-death situations to the complexities of life in the modern world. In a sense, because stress sets off an alarm system in our bodies, it can be very good for us and even save our life. We all face different challenges and problems, and stress motivates us to do our best and stay focused and alert.

The stress response

The stress, or 'fight-or-flight', response is automatic. We have all felt the range of dramatic symptoms that characterise this response: the heart pounding in the chest, the muscles tensing up, an increase in breathing rhythm, every sense on 'red alert'. These physical responses are matched at the emotional and mental levels: we must make decisions about what to do, while faced with feelings of panic, fear, or even anger.

The stress response begins in the brain, where danger is sensed or perceived. First, the hypothalamus sets off an electrochemical alarm. The sympathetic nervous system responds by initiating the release of hormones, including adrenaline and cortisone. The effect of these hormones on breathing is instantaneous; they speed up breathing so that larger quantities of oxygen are made available for the many processes set in motion by the stress response. The heartbeat increases so that more blood can flow to the large muscles, enabling us to run faster and fight harder; blood vessels near the skin constrict to prevent blood loss in the case of injury, and blood pressure is increased; our pupils dilate so that we can see better; more blood sugar is made available, especially by the liver, to release the necessary energy; and sweat is produced to cool the body. These stress effects all work together to speed up our reaction to the threat. At the same time, all bodily processes that are not essential to our immediate survival are slowed down or suppressed. The digestive and reproductive systems slow down, while growth hormone secretion and the immune response are inhibited.

When stress becomes a stressor

Although the fight-or-flight response has helped to protect us for many thousands of years, there are times when these responses are not of much benefit. Instead, the causes of stress – including the fears, anxieties and worries we think up within our own heads – either increase or do not stop. This happens when we cannot get away from the threat or we cannot deal with it. The threat then becomes a stressor.

Often the stress we feel is psychological rather than from physical threats. Psychological stressors are actually quite commonplace. Examples include caring for a sick or elderly person, day after day, with no end of their demands in sight; bills that mount up; sitting in heavy, slow-moving traffic; having a work deadline that seems impossible to meet; arguing with a loved one and wishing we had said something different; and arriving home after a long day at work and being confronted with negativity from others. Stressors such as these may make us feel exhausted, like we've had enough. We feel like this because our body puts us into automatic overdrive and our stress responses are constantly running. Further, the more the stress response is activated, the harder it becomes to turn it off. Instead of diminishing once a crisis has been dealt with, the stress response continues to trigger the release of stress hormones. Our breathing remains shallow and rapid, and our blood pressure remains high. The systems that have been slowed down remain sluggish, and the body now has to deal with the numerous side effects of the chemicals that have been poured into it.

Aside from stressors that are self-generated, many stressors are introduced into our lives by others. These can be environmental, family, and relationship stressors, as well as work and social stressors. It is worth noting that not all stress is caused by *negative* events. For example, the process of getting married can be highly stressful. However, according to psychologists, among the most common stressful life events are:

- The death of a loved one

- Marital problems

- Injury or illness

- Losing your job

- Moving house

- Money worries

- Dealing with legal situations

- Serving a prison sentence

The warning signs of stress

Stress affects us physically, emotionally and mentally. The first step in stress management is learning to recognise the warning signs of stress within ourselves. Stress behaviours may include changes in eating and/or sleeping habits; drug use, including alcohol and cigarettes, for relaxation; the development of nervous habits, for example coughing or tapping your feet on the floor; teeth grinding, especially during sleep; overreacting to situations; searching for distractions; and social isolation. Some physical effects may include headaches; backaches (a widespread reaction to stress); digestive disorders; chest pains; weight changes; skin problems (eczema being the most common); insomnia; and frequent immune system reactions such as colds. In terms of our emotions, we may feel moody, agitated, irritable, tense, overwhelmed and depressed. During times of stress, we also might notice changes in our mental state; we might exhibit difficulties in concentration, an inability to make decisions, poor judgement, negative attitudes, anxiety, fear, memory loss and other cognitive problems.

Those are just some of the vast range of warnings we give ourselves that something needs to be done to bring about change and alleviate our stress. The changes made may need to be instant, and some may need to be long-term. You already know if you are suffering from the impact of stress. However, it is important to remain mindful and aware of your internal state because one can normalise and ignore the effects of stress when they are ongoing. Furthermore, it is important to check out anything that is bothering you with a medical or health care professional. While the stress response is a universal survival technique, our reactions to stress are highly individual. Some are more able to cope with certain stressors than others. What might be a minor difficulty to others could be a daunting obstacle and a psychological pressure to you. You know what you can and cannot cope with and when you have reached your limit. Your body, mind and emotions will try to tell you when you are nearing or have reached your limit of tolerance. This is why I suggest you become acquainted with not only your reactions to stress but also the roots of your reactions.

Breathing to overcome stress: relaxation

You may have noticed that you breathe at your best when your body is fully relaxed. All through your day there are times when you would benefit from being able to relax, really deeply, at a moment's notice. However, simply sitting and resting or even taking a nap may not release the accumulated muscle tension that is created by stress. Your body needs to be 'told' that it is safe to relax and that this is what you are going to do. If not, your stressed body or anxious mind will stay in a state of readiness: for fight or flight.

Conscious relaxation combined with conscious breathing allows you to become aware of how, throughout the day, your body reacts to life events and stores related tension. This is particularly so when people are disconnected from or unaware of their bodies. You will find that conscious relaxation goes hand in hand with conscious breathing. This is because, when you make the intention to breathe consciously (as in carrying out any of the exercises), the heart energy centre, rather than the solar plexus, automatically takes control and the other centres follow the guidance of the heart centre.

Once this happens, the body's relaxation response relieves tension and stress, at all levels, and allows the body's energies to flow more freely. The activities of the brain, heart and lungs are slowed down, which calms the mind and emotions. Calming our emotions and steadying the mind creates the ideal state for self-healing.

Relaxation is a prerequisite for any balancing or healing work you wish to do on yourself, or another, and you now know that this is put in place whenever you place your attention in your heart centre. Finally, deep relaxation allows for detachment from the body, thus creating the perfect conditions for contemplation and/or meditation. Detachment from the body, in this way, also brings the benefits of reducing physical, emotional and mental pain. Thus, you will find it helpful, in so many ways, to be able to relax at will.

The next exercise is a simple yet thorough method of relaxing the whole body. In it you will send a command to your brain to allow all your muscles to relax, release and let go of tension. You can facilitate this relaxation with slow, deep and gentle breathing, which immediately sends positive messages to all the body systems that things are becoming calm and peaceful. Once your body and mind are acquainted with the feeling of relaxation, you will be able to move into relaxation mode at will. This will be an essential element in your preparation for any breathing exercise. It will also become a useful life skill.

EXERCISE 13

Full-body relaxation

You may find it useful to record the following exercise first and play it back, or have it read out to you by a partner. You may recall from Exercise 3 (Breathing to support your back, page 31) how breathing via the nose helps induce the body's relaxation response, but when you want to let go of any worries or anxieties it is helpful, initially, to let go of them via the breath through the open mouth. The secret here is not to *try* to relax. Your muscles know how to do it. Simply let go of the tension in your muscles each time you exhale.

The exercise takes some space to explain, but it is simply about relaxing every joint and muscle in your body, beginning at one end of your body and working your way to the other end.

- Choose a clean, firm and even surface with a comfortable support for your head and neck, such as a small pillow or cushion.

- Lie down on your back and check that your head and neck are comfortable. Allow your legs to part slightly and move your hands away from the sides of your body.

- Carry out the deep full-breath breathing of Exercise 2 (page 28) three times. Let any problems or anxieties go with your out-breath, breathing them out through an open mouth.

- When you feel you have let go of any anxious feelings, close your mouth and breathe slowly, gently and normally through your nose.

exercise continues ▶

- Bring your focus to your hands. As you breathe in, clench them tightly to make a fist. As you breathe out, let them unclench. Repeat this. Breathe in, and clench your fists. Let them unclench as you breathe out. Remember this feeling of unclenching and letting go as you exhale. This is how you relax.

- Do not clench anything again throughout the rest of this exercise. As you breathe in, know that you are breathing in peace and relaxation. As you breathe out, know that you are relaxing and letting go.

- Bring your focus to the toes of your left foot. Feel them relax, one by one. Use the out-breath to let them release and relax. Move your attention slowly over your foot, relaxing the muscles. Let the ankle go.

- Move your attention up your left leg, relaxing the muscles in time with your breathing. Let the knee joint go. Relax the thigh muscles and the muscles of the buttocks.

- Relax your pelvis. Continue to breathe slowly and gently.

- Now focus on your right foot. Feel your toes relax, one by one. Move your attention slowly over your right foot, relaxing the muscles, letting go. Relax your ankle joint.

- Move your attention up your right leg and let the knee joint go. Relax the thigh muscles and the muscles of the buttocks. Relax your pelvis again.

- Now move your attention up the front of your body, relaxing the belly and stomach. Let go of the muscles of the chest. Let go of your shoulders.

- Return your attention to your lower back and slowly relax your back muscles. Use the out-breath to let go of any muscular tension. If you suffer from back pain, make sure you take the time to relax all of the back muscles. Pay attention to the

exercise continues ▶

muscles across the top of your back and shoulders where tension tends to gather. Relax and let go.

- Relax your left shoulder and move down the left arm. Relax your elbow joint. Move down the forearm, relaxing and letting go, in time with your breathing. Let your wrist relax.

- Relax the palm of your left hand, thumb and fingers, one by one.

- Return your attention to your right shoulder. Relax it and move down the right arm. Let your elbow joint relax. Move down your forearm, relaxing and letting go. Let your wrist relax.

- Relax your right hand, letting go of your thumb and fingers one by one. Relax your entire shoulder girdle.

- Now move up the back of your neck, very slowly, relaxing and letting go. Let your attention come up the back of your head and over the top of the scalp, relaxing and letting go of all the tiny muscles.

- Imagine a caring hand smoothing your forehead. As you exhale, relax your eyes, the cheeks, and your mouth. Relax your jaw.

- Continue to breathe slowly, gently and normally. Now mentally scan your body to see if any part has tensed up again. If it has, relax it, enjoying the feeling of total relaxation and letting go. At this point you can remain mentally alert or allow yourself to drift off into sleep.

When you feel ready, open your eyes and wiggle your toes. Allow yourself to be totally conscious of your body before you stand up.

When you repeat this exercise, try starting the relaxation at the top of your body, making your way down to the toes, using the same techniques. See which order is most comfortable for you. You may find that you need to use a different order to suit different times or circumstances. Practise this relaxation exercise, or some form of it, until it becomes second nature and you can do it anywhere, in any circumstance, in any position. Conscious relaxation, like conscious breathing, re-establishes a positive relationship with every aspect of your body.

Benefits of the relaxation response

Regular practice of the above relaxation exercise – once a week or whenever you feel tense – will also bring you mental relaxation. Every time you practise the relaxation exercise, it will become progressively easier to allow the flow of thoughts through your mind without your needing to grasp any of them. With practise, your mind begins to empty itself. This is perfectly normal and is an important outcome of combining relaxation with your breathing. Conscious breathing and relaxation are one of the most effective ways to cope with any stressful situation. Begin by practising Exercise 2: Full-breath breathing and then Exercise 13: Full-body relaxation (above). These two exercises initiate the relaxation response, the antidote to the stress response.

In deep relaxation, when your breathing becomes slower and deeper, your brain gets the message that it can put a brake on the fight-or-flight state of hormone alert. Very quickly, your heart rate decreases, your blood pressure drops or stabilises, your muscles relax, and all the body systems resume their normal functioning. Because stress overload depletes the body's reserves, your body can now begin the restoration process. Where excessive hormone secretion has pro-duced chemical imbalance, your body immediately works to recover balance. Many of these physical reactions also have a positive effect on your emotional and mental attitudes and equilibrium.

The sacred impulse between the breaths

Stress concentrates the mind on the threat to our survival so that we are forced to focus on the body – how we are feeling, and how to alleviate the situation. During times of stress, then, we may lose sight of our link with our spiritual reality. But conscious breathing will quickly re-establish this link. When the communication link with the Source is made, it is reflected in the breath as an energetic rhythm: a pulsation that occurs between breaths.

The following exercise will restore your natural breathing rhythm and prepare your respiratory system to await the arrival of this sacred energetic impulse between breaths. This allows the use of rhythmic breathing to reinforce the beneficial side effects of efficient breathing (such as a decrease in heart rate, a stabilisation of blood pressure, total muscular relaxation and the resumption of normal functioning in all the body systems), and to affirm the presence of the higher self within you. You effectively restore the Breath of Unity.

EXERCISE 14

Rhythmic breathing

For best results, record the exercise and play it back, or have a partner read it to you.

- Sit comfortably in a chair with your feet flat on the ground. Notice your breathing. Allow it to become slow, deep and gentle.

- Practise full-breath breathing for three complete breaths. Check to see if you are relaxed, paying attention to the muscles of your pelvic and shoulder girdles and the back of your neck.

- Now inhale to a count of three. Hold for a count of one. Exhale to a count of three. Hold for a count of one. Do this for three breathing cycles.

- See if you can inhale to a count of four. Hold for a count of two. Exhale to a count of four. Hold for a count of two. Breathe to this rhythm for six breaths. Do not strain.

- As you grow relaxed and confident with the four/two rhythm, see if you can increase it to six/three without straining.

Within the pause between breaths lies all potential, all possibility, everything you need at this time. Within the pause is the presence and awareness of your higher self, the 'I am'. Within this place of calmness, nervousness, fear, or anxiety do not exist. This exercise may be practised whenever you feel the onset of stress.

Of course, breathing accompanies our every action and is not something confined to our being still. Walking is a great way to relieve stress. But very often, in the stressed state, we take little notice of our breathing. Here is a fun way of taking notice of our breath and then introducing a rhythm to the simple but beneficial activity of walking.

EXERCISE 15

The Walking Breath

The exercise is best practised outdoors, preferably away from traffic, but you could run through it indoors first.

- Get used to walking at a relaxed pace and notice the way you are breathing. Next try walking at different speeds and in different ways. What happens to your breathing?

- Now introduce a breathing rhythm to your favourite way of relaxed walking. Inhale to a count of four. Hold for a count of two. Exhale for a count of six. Hold for a count of two. Inhale again for a count of four. And so on.

- When you feel used to this simple rhythm, inhale to a count of four, hold for a count of two, and exhale to a count of eight. Check that your breathing rhythm and your walking rhythm are in harmony with each other.

The Walking Breath reminds you how you can enjoy the simple pleasure of walking. Once your breathing rhythm and walking rhythms are in harmony you can forget them and become aware of your surroundings, the way the commonplace may now reveal fascinating details that you never really noticed before. Establishing your link with the Breath of Unity in this way opens your awareness to the energies of your surroundings. You are open to feel your surroundings and feel how your body is positively adjusting to the absence of stress.

The next exercise helps counter the effects of negative news and attitudes on your subtle energy system.

EXERCISE 16

Breathing to counter the effects of negative energies

All news and information, from all forms of media, have energy. So do the attitudes of others. Energy that is not conducive to our own well-being may be termed 'negative' because of its effect on us. When confronted with what we sense as 'negative', a powerful counterstrategy is to find our place in the heart centre and use this point of reference to rebalance the system. This is often more empowering for us than denial or flight from confrontation. Empowerment is always a facet of self-healing.

During the exercise, breathing takes you to the heart centre as the key centre in the breathing process, the balancing point in the subtle energy system and the centre which is 'listened to' by all the other centres.

- Sit comfortably in a chair with your feet flat on the ground. Rest your hands on your thighs, palms up (in receptive mode). Breathe normally. Relax your elbows, the back of your neck, and the tops of your shoulders. Do this by letting go of muscle tension with each out-breath. Close your eyes if this helps you concentrate.

- Breathe into your heart centre. As you do so, visualise a green light in your heart centre that gets brighter each time you

exercise continues ▶

inhale. Allow the green light to fill up your heart centre and to move out into the area around it.

- Let your focus move slowly and gently down to your solar plexus centre. Visualise a golden yellow light as you inhale. Allow this light to fill up your solar plexus and the area of the body around it.

- Now let your focus move slowly and gently down to your sacral centre. Visualise a bright orange light as you inhale. Let this light fill up your sacral centre and the area of the body around it.

- Let your focus move down to your base centre. Visualise a bright red light as you inhale. Allow the light to fill up your base centre and the body around it.

- Return your focus to your heart centre. See the green light awaiting you. Let your focus slowly and gently rise to your throat centre. Visualise a sky-blue light as you inhale. Allow this light to fill up your throat centre and the areas of your throat, nose and ears.

- Let your focus gently rise to your brow centre. Visualise a royal blue or indigo light as you inhale. Let this light fill up your brow centre and your head and eyes.

- Finally, let your focus slowly rise to your crown centre. Visualise a violet light as you inhale. Allow this light to fill up your crown centre, covering the top of your head.

- Return your focus to your heart centre. See the green light awaiting you again. Relax and breathe naturally.

Once you have mastered the exercise, you might like to try it as another form of the Walking Breath to relieve stress. It may be practised as an alternative to, or in conjunction with, Exercise 14: Rhythmic Breathing.

Stress-relief and your daily routine

If you have been, or still are, going through a stressful period, it would be wise to make rhythmic breathing part of your daily routine, and schedule to do it once or twice a day. If you have the chance, also include the Walking Breath. First thing in the morning is the best time to do your stress-relief practice so that you start your day with your body and mind in a calm, balanced state. However, if you practise at night, just before you go to bed, it will provide the basis for sound sleep. Remember that all the breathing exercises should be done in as quiet an environment as possible; your posture should be comfortable with your back straight, and close your eyes or gently focus on something in your surroundings. Most importantly, don't worry about your thoughts and the fact that they appear. Simply allow them to pass through your mind. You have trained your mind to think, so try not to blame yourself for your thoughts. They are not you.

Take notice of how stress has led you to change your attitudes about yourself and how you view other people and the life around you. Your attitudes determine your perspective on life, how you see others, and how you react to the stressors that come your way. During your deep-breathing sessions, take time in your relaxed state to do this. Where did your attitudes originate? Did you learn them from others or did you create them yourself? Simply recognising them will allow you to change them if you feel they are not enhancing your life. Use your healing journal to make notes about your findings and perhaps to decide what attitudes you would like to change.

In the next chapter we move from stress to serenity with the time-honoured antidote to stress: breathing meditation.

Chapter 6

Breathing and meditation

The transformation of the mind

From infancy, when we first interact with family, caregivers and our surroundings, we begin to develop attitudes and perspectives that will determine how we react to other people and situations. Our mind is programmed to be trained, and we do this unconsciously. Our mindsets are a result of this training. By the time we reach adolescence, we are responding to life through our programmed mindsets, or we are challenging them aggressively. One day as adults, perhaps many years later, we realise that some of our attitudes and perspectives are not serving us and that they are actually hindering what we want to express, thwarting opportunities and spoiling relationships. Our life is not playing out as we want it to be.

These feelings signal that we have lost touch with who we really are and we have lost touch with our connection to the sacred. But the good news is that, because the mind is programmed to be trained, it can be retrained – we can wake up to what has been happening to us. The Buddha (c.563–c.483 BCE) was once asked when a person should attempt such retraining of the mind. He replied: 'There is only one moment in time when it is essential to awaken and that moment is now.' The simple awakening method that he recommended is known as breathing meditation.

The Dalai Lama, of the Tibetan Buddhist tradition, describes meditation as the transformation of the mind. It means that, through meditation, powerful mindsets can be changed or even eliminated. Our inherited or early-formed mindsets will no longer dictate how and what we will think, how we will speak and what we will say, or how we will act and what we will do. Instead, we will be able to take control of these aspects of our life. This is one of the main goals of meditation. Meditation practices aid in transformation. They give us the *power* to bring about mental change. But, as the Dalai Lama warns, when we practise breathing meditation we must not forget that if we do not change the way we think, speak and act, meditation will not do it for us.

Transformations of heart and mind through meditation

Through the practice of breathing meditation, the most important transformation is the cultivation of the heart centre, the centre of compassion and the wisdom of the soul. Getting in touch with your heart centre allows you to not simply witness the pain of others, but to empathise with it and try to alleviate it. When you witness the pain or distress of others, with your mind in your heart centre, breathe out to them. Make a conscious link with them through your breath.

A second transformation which can occur through the regular practice of breathing meditation is that you begin to realise that we are all One, that all humans are the same, and that all humans are here to manifest their spiritual reality. When you are aware of the struggles of others to truly be themselves, breathe out to them from your heart centre, making a conscious link with them through your breath.

Once you truly absorb the realisation that all humans are One, you become aware that you are also One with the animal, plant and mineral worlds, and that they too are here to manifest their spiritual reality. When you become aware of an animal or plant in distress, you can breathe out to them, making a conscious link with them through your breath. Similarly, when you become aware of disruption to any landscape, or your own environment, you can breathe out to these places, making a conscious link with them through your breath.

Breathing awareness, when linked to meditation practice, will help to strengthen, energise and encourage you to bring about positive changes in yourself and the world around you. How far you are able to do this, and how far you are able to express who you really are, will go hand in hand with your progress in the kind of self-transformations mentioned above.

The experience of Oneness

For many who meditate, the transformation of the mind is a vital first step towards moving into a state of consciousness where mental activity is stilled and where the mind seems to disappear. For Buddhists, this is known as 'Buddha consciousness', or 'no-mind'. For yogis, it is the state of *samadhi*, 'Atman consciousness', or consciousness of the higher self. The Gnostics called this experience *gnosis*, or a deep inner knowing, stressing that it had nothing to do with intellectual knowledge. Each tradition uses different language to describe this natural and universal experience. In my own life, I describe conscious alignment with the Source as the experience of Oneness. Even before such experiences, you can remember your moment-by-moment oneness with the Source through the Breath of Unity, through every breath you take.

Experiences of Oneness can occur at any moment and cannot usually be anticipated or planned. Typically, they may be quite simple, but they are vivid, unforgettable, and often accompanied by a sense of oneness with everything that is being felt, seen and sensed. Many people also report being enveloped in a profound sense of joy. Most of us can remember having such experiences, but not everyone gives them much regard.

The first Oneness experience that I can recall happened when I was three as a dream vision in that place between sleep and waking. My second experience occurred at the age of eight while exploring a forest with a young school friend. It is usual for a person to have many Oneness experiences and each experience tends to deepen the effects of the one before.

Linking with the higher self

We need to remember that the mind alone cannot know the higher self any more than it can know the Source (God), hence the perennial problem of defining the experience of 'inner knowing'. The mind's conditioning stands in the way of our linking with the higher self. It therefore needs to change its awareness and viewpoint, from that of a conditioned personality alone, to a soul operating through and with the personality. Meditation is transcendental when it takes us beyond the limitations of mind, beyond thought, to encounter who we really are: the spiritual, higher self.

When the purpose of meditation is to link with the higher self and the spiritual Source, this can only take place once the mind is still. All effective meditation techniques lead to this calming of the mind. In doing so, meditation allows the personality to make contact with the soul, providing a channel for soul expression. Balance, harmony and vitality return once the connection with our reason for coming to the planet has been revealed to us again. Meditation is thus one of the great self-healing techniques.

The effects of meditation

In the meditative state, the mind relaxes and the electrical activity of the brain's cerebral cortex moves out of the rhythm of everyday consciousness, the so-called beta rhythm. It assumes a new rhythm that is either close to the delta rhythm of the sleep state, known as 'slow-wave sleep', or the alpha rhythm of wakeful relaxation. The bodily processes, under the control of the autonomic nervous system, such as breathing and heartbeat, slow down considerably. This allows our consciousness to move away from the physical to the subtle levels and ultimately to connect with soul consciousness.

There are great benefits from calming the mind and the emotions. The senses are sharpened, giving greater access to intelligence and inner wisdom. The body appreciates the time you take to meditate and the way you engage in deep and gentle breathing to slow down the heartbeat and calm all of the body's systems. This is how breathing meditation is a great antidote to stress and the effects of stress, and why it has become an important element in many stress management and relaxation programmes.

These positive effects act on the levels of mind and emotion to release stored negative and other unwanted energies. Repressed emotional and mental material may be stored in any part of the physical body and in the energy centres. Meditation has the power to unlock these energies and bring renewed energy flow. This may be felt as one or more of a range of sensations, from small involuntary body movements to tingling, heat and heightened perceptions. Energy release may even be accompanied by the need to shout or vocalise in some way. Such releases of energy are quite normal and nothing to be alarmed about. People who meditate also report an increase in vitality, the curing of a range of physical conditions and a return to balance, lightness and well-being.

Compassion and wisdom

Compassion is a power of the heart, not just a wish that others may be free from their suffering. As well as the practice of breathing meditation, you can further access this transforming energy by becoming close with others and empathising with them. Once you have walked a mile in someone's moccasins, as Native Americans have put it, you soon see the need for loving kindness rather than judgement and condemnation. In the beginning stages, compassion cannot be developed in a general way – 'I feel sorry for the people of ...', for example. Instead, focus on an actual person, even if that person is a TV image. To develop the power of focusing on another, breathe out to them from your heart centre. Consciously link with them via your breathing.

We are able to access the wisdom of the heart once we start the process of bringing our minds to see things as they really are. This is done by gradually challenging our own conditioned or prejudiced perceptions of reality. Our attitudes and perspectives are, of course, a reflection of our mindsets. As your mindset presents itself, and this can happen at any moment without warning, breathe it into your heart centre, accepting it with your breath and realising that your breath can help in bringing about change.

The three stages of breathing meditation

In the meditative state we are wholly conscious and aware, with the mind as still as possible. If prayer can be described as a talking mode, meditation is a listening mode. In this sense, the person meditating does not carry on an internal dialogue but sits calmly and patiently. It is more important to be in the process of meditating rather then to expect some sort of outcome or benefit. Meditation is a state of being and not a state of expectation or achievement.

It is helpful to think of meditation as having three stages. The first is *concentration*, or finding a suitable focus for the mind. Once the mind is comfortably focused, you move to the second stage, *contemplation*. This happens when the flow of concentration is uninterrupted and the focus unfolds itself of its own volition. At this stage the mind is still involved, but is gradually becoming less active as thoughts and distractions are simply allowed to pass through. This is a position of great strength and stillness and many healing benefits are obtained during this stage. With practise, the mind is totally calmed and the link with soul consciousness is made as the third stage is reached: the *meditative state*. During healing, advanced spiritual healers enter a very similar state to the meditative state and they are often able to communicate or transfer this special state of mind to the patient.

Techniques leading to the meditative state

Meditation is a convenient label for a range of techniques and it should not become a dogma. It would be far more accurate to describe meditation as a way of being. It is being with your self, and being your higher self. For some this may happen when sitting quietly. For others, the meditative state occurs when the body is moving, such as when walking in nature, when working, when immersed in a creative task, when playing music, or when dancing. Acts of service can be deep forms of meditation. When you are in love with someone, and you suddenly sense there is only one of you, being with your beloved becomes an experience of Oneness, taking you to the meditative state.

There are many techniques which can still the mind and lead to the meditative state. A photo, diagram, picture, or symbol may be the starting point of a visual focus of attention. Visualisation is a simple and common method where imagery provides the focus and subject for contemplation. For example, the technique could take you to that peaceful place where you are totally relaxed and calm so that the mind gradually becomes stilled. You can imagine such a place or recall one that you have been to. Chanting, aloud or internally, or sounds made with instruments, also act as powerful focuses, their energies often designed to still the mind and help in its transformation.

Many religions have evolved methods of contemplation which may or may not lead to meditation, according to whether the intention is to still the mind. Some of these methods have led to confusion over meaning. For example, if you contemplate a text, mulling over its implications and so on, you are not entering the third stage of meditation because the mind is still active. If, however, your focus on the text leads to a point where you stop contemplating and simply wait, without any expectations, you may well move into the meditative state.

The practice described in this book for reaching the meditative state is breathing meditation, with its focus in the heart centre.

Establishing a programme for meditation

Some people need a ritual to get them in the right mood for meditation. Anything which tells the mind that this is what is on your agenda is going to be useful. Once you have mastered a technique, you will be able to meditate anywhere and at any time, no matter what is going on around you. Until then, do whatever helps you to create the mood.

Choose a regular time to meditate. Dawn and dusk are particularly good because the world around us seems to enter into a special tranquillity, a phase of balance, at these times. More important is to give the mind notice that at such and such a time you are going to meditate.

Choose a regular place. If possible this should be set aside for meditation. It should be kept clean and fresh. You might like to keep a candle there, even a little shrine. Lighting a candle, dedicating it, dedicating yourself and your work, prayers, lighting incense – these are all signals to the mind that you want it to cooperate with you and honour this sacred time and space.

Choosing a comfortable way to sit

Sit comfortably. It is important to be comfortable, with the back straight and the hands resting on the thighs. Your hands may rest on your thighs either palms up or palms down and this position depends on your intention. When your palms are held upwards, their energy centres are available to receive subtle information. When they are held in the downwards position you are focusing on inner events alone.

It has not been proved that the lotus position is the most effective position for meditation, though it is the preferred position in most Asian countries for cultural and religious reasons. An attitude of joy in just sitting, in just being, without expectation, is essential to true meditation. In China and Japan the meditation position is known as 'sitting like a mountain'. This gives the right feeling of solidity and stillness, with the body well connected to the ground and the mind reaching to the heavens. When you sit, having this image of yourself will be very helpful to your practice.

Choose your comfortable sitting position. When sitting on a chair, your elbows and shoulders should be relaxed with your head held erect. Make sure your feet are flat on the ground and your back straight, your legs uncrossed with your hands resting gently on your thighs. The uncrossed position of the legs ensures a proper connection between the soles of your feet and the ground. If you prefer to sit on the ground, it is just as effective to sit in a comfortable cross-legged position because in that position your base centre is able to make direct contact with the ground. This allows the base centre to act in the same way as the soles of the feet as an energetic grounding point.

The meditation exercises below are designed to help you access higher levels of consciousness. Your energetic grounding point ensures that you always return to your *physical* body and *physical* consciousness, simply and safely, at the end of the exercise. In my first experience, I was not aware that I was 'out of my body' until I 'came back into it'. This is because the transition from the physical to other levels is seamless. The feeling of 'coming back' was somewhat like returning to the ground floor in a lift. Once you are aware of the process, moving back to body consciousness can be almost instantaneous, but it does not have to be rushed – your energetic grounding point will ensure that your consciousness returns to

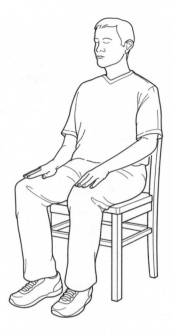

Figure 9: The meditation position

'normal'. Movements, such as rubbing parts of the body and flexing your fingers and toes, all aid the process.

When meditation is a spiritual act and a spiritual discipline, it puts us in touch with the source of healing energies. It puts us in touch with the network of consciousness, linking us to our body, and all other beings. Even five minutes of meditation is five minutes when we treat ourselves to being at one with all things.

Breathing – a powerful focus for meditation

In its simplest form, meditation is simply being still, on every level, and the world's traditions offer us many forms of being still. When you recall that breathing is driven by the heart centre and that the heart centre is the place of access to all healing energies, it is not surprising that working with the breath is the most time-honoured meditation technique. Moreover, breathing meditation arises from its simplicity – the breath is always with us.

Traditionally, there are several locations of your body where you can concentrate your awareness on the breath. Because it is considered to be the place of the soul, the heart centre is the preferred centre of focus for healing purposes, as well as for establishing our communication link with the Breath of Unity. By breathing into the heart centre, you will be able to keep your focus there and you will be able to return to it throughout the day, even when you are doing other tasks, resting, or relaxing.

Three forms of breathing meditation practice follow. Try each form to see which form is the most comfortable or appealing for you. Exercise 17 is the simplest form and is followed by counting your breaths (Exercise 18) and following the sound of your breath (Exercise 19).

EXERCISE 17

Becoming one with your breath

Read the exercise through carefully until you are thoroughly familiar with it. You may find it helpful to record this exercise or have someone read it to you. Check that you have decided on your most comfortable sitting position.

- Sitting on a chair, or on the ground, place your palms over your heart centre (in the middle of your chest) for a few moments, to help you get a tangible sense of how your breath moves in this area. Allow your hands to rest on your thighs, either palms up or palms down.

- Let your body sway gently from side to side three to six times to reach a point of balance.

- If possible, breathe through your nose. Notice how you breathe in, the pause, and how you breathe out.

- Take six full breaths, and, as you relax your body, allow your shoulder girdle to drop and your pelvis to sink into the chair. Let your elbows relax. Check that no other part of your body is clenched or tight.

exercise continues ▶

- Now imagine that you are joining your breath, becoming one with your breath, rather than trying to observe or watch your breath the way you might watch something separate from yourself.

- Pay attention to the whole cycle of each breath. You may find at times that you have begun to tune out during the last part of the exhalation. When you tune out, this gives your mind the opportunity to wander. With your focus on the complete movement of each breath, remain aware of the total experience of each breath. Observe how each inhalation becomes an exhalation and each exhalation becomes an inhalation. Observe the period between the exhalation and the inhalation.

- Do not try to stop your mind from thinking. When you realise that you are thinking, let go of your thoughts the way you let go of your breath when you exhale. This flexibility, this ability to drop distraction and return to the breath, again and again, is one of the most important elements in practising breathing meditation. The ability to let go is essential. It will enable you to let go of your attitudes, your opinions, your irritations and anger, your pain, your regrets, and your grief. Whether we like it or not, change is inevitable. Breathing meditation gives us the opportunity to practise letting go of the past now.

- In the initial stages of your practice, your attention may wander because the mind is programmed to generate thoughts. When you notice that you are distracted – perhaps remembering the past, planning the future, or involved in an emotional state, or even about to fall asleep – wake yourself up. Without forcing yourself, try to be aware of the present moment and your full presence right where you are.

- The aim of this exercise is not to keep a blank or empty mind. Nor is it to force your attention on to your breath. That would lead to an inflexible state of mind. Rather, your practice will lead to a flexible state of mind by helping you let go whenever

exercise continues ▶

you notice that you are distracted from your intention to engage with the present. Be ready to let go of distractions, to let go of insights, to let the busy mind stop and to return to your breath.

- With practise, you will realise that you have entered the meditative state without trying. The movement of your breathing may seem to have stopped, as 'you' and your body awareness seem to fade. You have come face to face with your higher self as you are now totally aware of Oneness.

- When you feel that your meditation session is over, return to your body consciousness calmly and deliberately. Become aware of your surroundings, your feet, and your contact with the ground. Wiggle your toes and fingers. Give your thighs a vigorous rub. Give thanks.

Initially, carry out the exercise for five minutes. When you are able to maintain a strong, prolonged focus, extend this time to eight or ten minutes. Over time, build this up to twenty or thirty minutes.

When you practise breathing meditation, your mind follows your breathing. The air comes in and goes out. When your mind is calm enough to follow the movement of your breath, you may think: I am breathing, I can hear the sound of my breath, I am one with the Breath of Unity. Eventually you will discover that there is no 'you' to say 'I am breathing'. There is no I, no world, no mind, no body. All that exists is the Breath of Unity. You will find that this total, unconditional awareness is central to meditation practice.

EXERCISE 18

Counting the breath

Carefully read the exercise through until you are thoroughly familiar with it. You may find it helpful to record this exercise or have someone read it to you.

- Sitting on a chair, or on the ground, as in the previous exercise, place your palms over your heart centre for a few moments, to help you get a tangible sense of how your breath moves in this area. Allow your hands to rest on your thighs, either palms up or palms down.

- Let your body sway gently from side to side three to six times to reach a point of balance.

- If possible, breathe through your nose. Notice how you breathe in, the pause, and how you breathe out.

- Take six full breaths, and, as you relax your body, allow your shoulder girdle to drop and your pelvis to sink into the chair. Let your elbows relax. Check that no other part of your body is tense.

- Now begin to count each exhalation, in your mind, until you reach 'ten'. Start another count to ten with your next exhalation. Continue with this form of breathing meditation practice.

- Each count is aligned with the natural breathing rhythm. Your breath should lead the counting. If you practise counting your breath, with time you will find that you will be able to maintain counting while your attention has drifted elsewhere. If you are counting and find that you have gone beyond ten, stop counting, and with your next exhalation begin again with one. The same is true when you notice that you are lost in your thoughts; start counting again, beginning with one.

exercise continues ▶

- Now imagine that, as you count each breath, you are joining your breath, becoming one with your breath, rather than observing or watching your breath from the outside.

- Do not try to stop your mind from thinking. When you realise that you are thinking, let go of your thoughts the way you let go of your breath when you exhale. This ability to drop distraction and return to the count of your breaths, again and again, is one of the most important elements in practising breathing meditation. The ability to let go is essential and breathing meditation gives us the opportunity to practise this.

- In the initial stages of your practice, your attention may wander because the mind is programmed to generate thoughts. When you notice that you are distracted, try to become aware of the present moment and your full presence right where you are.

- The aim of this exercise is not to keep a blank or empty mind. Nor is it to force your attention on to your breath or the number of your counts. Rather, the aim is to create a flexible state of mind by helping you let go whenever you notice that you are distracted from your intention to engage with the present. Let go of distractions, let go of insights, let the busy mind stop, and return to your breath.

- With practise, you will realise that you have entered the meditative state without trying. The movement of your breathing may seem to have stopped, as 'you' and your body awareness seem to fade. You have come face to face with your higher self as you are now totally aware of Oneness.

- When you feel that your meditation session is over, return to your body consciousness calmly and deliberately. Become aware of your surroundings, your feet, and your contact with the ground. Wiggle your toes and fingers, and give your thighs a rub. Give thanks.

exercise continues ▶

Initially, carry out the exercise for five minutes. When you are able to maintain a strong, prolonged focus, extend this time to eight or ten minutes. Over time, build this up to twenty or thirty minutes.

In the third form of breathing meditation, you will follow and become one with the *sound* of your breathing.

EXERCISE 19

Becoming one with the sound of your breath

As before, carefully read the exercise through until you are thoroughly familiar with it. You may find it helpful to record this exercise or have someone read it to you.

- Sitting on a chair, or on the ground, let your body sway gently from side to side three to six times to reach a point of balance. Take six full breaths, as you relax your body, and allow your shoulder girdle to drop and your pelvis to sink into the chair. Let your elbows relax. Check that every part of your body is relaxed.

- Place the tips of your fingers over your brow centre (in the centre of your forehead, just above the eyes) for a few moments. This will be your focus area for this exercise. Lower your hands and place them gently back on your thighs, with your palms up.

- If possible, breathe through your nose. Notice how you breathe in, the pause, and how you breathe out.

- Pay attention to the sound of your breathing and the sound of each part of your breath.

exercise continues ▶

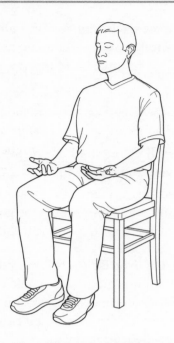

Figure 10: The meditation position – palms up

- When you have become familiar with the sound of your breathing, allow your focus to move to your brow centre and your 'inner screen'. (This is what you see with your eyes closed when you focus on your brow centre.) Relax, and stare at your inner screen, while remaining aware of the sound of your breath. Do not try to see anything on your inner screen; simply wait patiently until something appears.

- When something does appear on your inner screen, do not attempt to grasp at it because it will immediately disappear. Simply watch like an uninvolved observer. The aim is to merge with the sound of your breath, to become one with the sound of your breath, as you calmly watch your inner screen.

- When you notice that you are distracted – that you are thinking, remembering something, or falling asleep – wake up.

exercise continues ▶

Without forcing yourself, try to stay alert to the present moment, to your full presence, right where you are.

- With practise, you will realise that you have entered the meditative state without trying. The sound of your breathing may seem to have stopped, as 'you' seem to fade. Your inner screen has disappeared too, but you are totally aware of Oneness. You have come face to face with your higher self.

- When you feel that your meditation session is over, return to your body consciousness. Become aware of your surroundings, your feet, and your contact with the ground. Wiggle your toes and fingers. Give your thighs a rub. Give thanks.

Initially, carry out the exercise for five minutes. When you are able to maintain a strong, prolonged focus, extend this time to eight or ten minutes. Over time, build this up to twenty or thirty minutes.

Having practised these three distinct forms of breathing meditation, and perhaps choosing one form as your main practice, you should be aware of any problems which may have arisen and how to deal with them.

Dealing with meditation problems

Trying hard to be consciously aware of an involuntary action, like breathing, can produce tension and even an uncomfortable degree of self-consciousness. This is often the case when practising with a group. Sometimes, even though your breath is moving smoothly, you may feel as if you aren't getting enough oxygen; your breath may feel stuck as if you cannot breathe past a point in your upper chest. When sensations like these occur, consciously relax your body, forget about your breath, and return your attention to your posture, to your spine, to the feel of your hands on your thighs and other physical sensations, until you find that you are breathing normally again.

In breathing meditation, the goal is not to separate yourself from your experience in order to observe it. The Zen master Thich Nhat Hanh teaches that, although breathing meditation exercises might be described as following or watching the breath, the way to observe something in meditation is to *become* the thing we are observing, by removing the boundary between subject and object. In breathing meditation you have the opportunity to experience that the body and mind are one. You and the object of your meditation are also one.

Your reactions to any problem in meditation should not be taken as any kind of setback. They are your personality struggling with the idea that 'you' are more than your personality, more than the information about you that is stored in your mind's memory. Before your personality and its ego allow you to be self *and* higher self, they will try to solve the perceived lack of data by involving you in a variety of distractions.

In the early stages of meditation practice, you may be acutely aware of distractions. If you anticipate this, you won't be so unsettled by them when they happen. For example, you will be acutely aware of your body. It may itch or develop a pain. Acknowledge how you feel about the pain and then let your feeling go. Instead, be with the pain or discomfort. When you can do this, you will find that it no longer bothers you.

During your meditation practice, you will become aware of sounds. Some sounds, especially the human voice, can be very insistent visitors to your awareness. Just be aware of them and let them go. I advise my workshop participants to imagine any sound they hear as accompanying them in their meditation rather than distracting them from it.

All these problems – sounds, thoughts, pain, feelings – may sidetrack your meditation. They are the mind's way of trying to interest you, as a personality, in other things. In a sense, it clamours for your attention: 'Hello, I'm here!' Think of your mind as a dog or a horse that needs to be trained. You have always been the trainer. From now on, you will be kind yet firm with your mind. Let all your meditation problems go or simply let them be with you as you meditate.

Your mind has served your personality well. Now you want it to serve your spiritual self at the same time. The ego/personality is freed when, undisturbed by previous conditioning programmes and our emotional reactions, the mind returns to its pristine state – i.e., close to its state at conception, unencumbered by learned attitudes and perceived notions. This enables us to have a deeper experience of love and peace. Free from distracting thoughts, we can enter a deep silence. We can connect with a sense of internal clarity; we can feel open, relaxed and accepting. When the mind reaches this harmonious state, thoughts may arise, but they do not interfere with our clarity and harmony as they pass through our awareness. We become more open-hearted and willing to be present in the now; we are no longer lingering in, hankering after, or worrying about the past or the future. In this way, all aspects of self are brought into harmony.

Breathing meditation and the last breath

Our breathing, birth and death are connected. At birth, the breath helps us create, as a physical being, what we have brought from the spiritual realm. The life force and spiritual energies are adjusted so that they are attuned to physical matter. At the moment of death, the breath helps us create, as subtle energy, what we will take over into the spiritual realm from our physical life.

With our last breath, our last thought will pass away. Breathing and thinking are connected and this is why our last thoughts are so important, for our final thoughts will shape the energies that we take with us into the spiritual realm. Our last thoughts have been shaped by the attitudes and perspectives we have developed during life. This takes us back to the opening paragraphs of this chapter.

After a session of breathing meditation, you may like to record in your healing journal whether you are happy or not with your current attitudes and perspectives. If you are not happy with them, breathing meditation has the power to help you make any necessary changes.

We do not know when we will breathe our last breath so it is a good idea to have a gentle preparation for this as part of your personal routine. A simple practice is to be mindful of your breath as the Breath of Unity while you are falling asleep. When you wake up, wake up with an awareness of how you are breathing the Breath of Unity, your moment-by-moment link with the Source. Being mindful of the breath in this way is a key component in all self-healing. When the time comes, this breath practice will help you calmly embrace the transition back to the spiritual realm of existence.

The insights you've gathered and internalised from breathing meditation will change the way you breathe, and whatever benefits follow can be accepted as a gift. Your insights and their benefits will help cultivate a state of mind that is free of expectations and that feels gratitude for something as simple as your next breath. Gratitude for any gift completes the energetic cycle of the gift, and gratitude is a very positive last thought. To express your gratitude, return to the Breath of Unity. As you inhale, imagine your breath as representing what you may have received. As you exhale, your breath gives out your thanks to the universe.

Chapter 7

The healing breath

Breathing at the heart of healing

The Apache chief Geronimo (1829–1909) is well known as a great warrior. What is less well known is that he used the power of the breath and sacred song to bring about the shamanic transformation that gave him the ability to heal. His chants and breathing exercises enabled him to 'become a spirit being and fly through the air'. Like all Native American holy persons and healers, Geronimo understood that healing was a gift from the Source, and that breathing links our physicality with our spirituality. Without any effort on our part, through the Breath of Unity we have a constant reminder of who we really are. Every breath tells us that we are One with all things and, above all, One with the Source. Thus breathing and the breath play a central role in all forms of healing, and an understanding and application of this role of the breath is as crucial now as it was in Geronimo's time.

In today's world, people are suffering from 'soul malaise', an ailment that can manifest as a number of physical, emotional and mental conditions, which are the outcome of living in a state of disconnection from the sacred. In most cases, people suffering from soul malaise are unaware of the root causes of their illness, distress, or discontent. Breathing has the power to open us up to this awareness by creating space in the mind where we can pause and take stock. In addition, breathing can open up the body and the subtle energy system so that we can take in healing energies. Once this process begins, a regular practice of breathing exercises can provide ways to build inner and outer strength, and maintain vitality and energetic protection.

Balance and imbalance

Life is about change, even when it appears to be static. The tree in winter may be termed 'dormant' but it is far from asleep. Changes taking place within the whole body of the tree become very evident in the following spring. Even familiar mountains and hills may look the same from year to year, but they are being steadily worn away by weathering and may even lose or gain height due to movements within the Earth. Nature abhors stasis. We are the same. Our bodies, and our emotional and mental states, change from moment to moment. Bodily changes can initiate mental and emotional changes and vice versa. While this constant change happens on so many levels, our brains and subtle energy centres monitor what is happening, how we are changing. Moment by moment, processes are put in place to maintain our physical and subtle balance.

Change is normal and essential to life, its evolution and transformation. But change that instigates a longer-term imbalance may prevent these possibilities. Instead of enhancing life, some changes can inhibit or diminish it. There are always times when we are so out of balance that our body, our thoughts, or our feelings, or all three, signal to us that we have to do something conscious to restore balance. Our souls are always overseeing what is going on in our life and if we are balanced or unbalanced. When we stray from our path of soul expression, or the reason why we came to planet Earth, our soul finds ways to let us know. Our souls communicate to us through the language of feelings, not our emotions, which is why it is so important for us to keep in touch with our feelings. The subtle difference between feelings and emotions is that feelings originate in the heart centre, the place of the soul, while emotions are created by the mind's interactions with what we are presented with in life.

When we choose not to listen to our feelings, our soul prompts the mind to speak to us. We know that something is wrong, somewhere. If we do little to investigate, the message passes to the body. Our body is our friend, but it has to make us aware of the message that something is out of balance. We may then develop physical conditions ranging from the minor to the severe. Throughout this whole period, our breathing will have undergone changes according to the rhythms of our state of imbalance (another reason to remain mindful of our breath). Specific breathing exercises can work on the causes of our stress, illness, unhappiness, or discontent in order to restore balance in our lives.

Breathing for self-healing and healers

Throughout this book you are working towards the goal of continuous and conscious full-breath breathing because this is the greatest physical manifestation of your unity with the Source. Breathing with a heart-centre focus, or attunement, is a way to reconnect with your most balanced state. In the next exercise, you will align yourself with the Source of healing as the ideal way to begin your own self-healing practice or any kind of health care.

EXERCISE 20

Preparation for self-healing, healing or other therapeutic practice

Attunement means tuning your consciousness to the Source (God), like tuning a radio to receive a certain station. Breathing attunement is a simple and effective way to do this. You are able to disengage from the outside world and to engage with the inner world of your higher self. The three components of this attunement exercise are effective posture, effective breathing and effective focus, during which you are relaxed, yet fully aware. The exercise may be practised sitting on a chair or on the floor.

exercise continues ▶

- Sit in a chair so that the two girdles of the pelvis and shoulders are in line. Your spine should be straight; refrain from pushing your chest forward. Hold your head up without straining. Rest your hands, palms up, on your thighs. Have your feet flat on the floor, feeling your connection with the ground. This is your connection with the Earth. (Again, when sitting cross-legged on the floor, this connection is made via your base centre.)

- Using your breath, relax your body. With each out-breath, feel yourself relaxing and sinking into your pelvis. Relax your shoulders and the back of your neck. Now close your eyes, while remaining totally alert.

- Breathe naturally, through your nose. Keep your mouth lightly closed with your jaw unclenched.

- Breathe gently into your abdomen and enjoy the feeling of being relaxed yet alert. Recall that your breath is your moment-by-moment connection with the Source.

- Bring your focus to your heart centre, the place of your soul or higher self. Allow yourself to be at one with your higher self. Spend a few moments in union with Oneness, recalling that your higher self is always at one with the Source.

- Allow all thoughts to pass through your mind unobstructed. Any sounds around you are simply the accompaniment to your attunement. You are in the world, but nothing disturbs you. You are at one with the Source.

- Having reached this state of attunement, give thanks for the opportunity to be used as a channel for healing or self-healing. Ask to be as pure a channel as possible. Ask for protection for yourself and for all people, beings and situations. Dedicate yourself and your therapeutic work and ask for it to be blessed. Add any other prayers you wish, aware that you and the Source are one.

exercise continues ▶

- Now gradually return your attention to your breathing and allow your consciousness to move back into your body. When you feel ready, open your eyes, wiggle your toes, and become aware of your body before you stand up. Use your breathing to keep your focus in your heart centre.

From the attuned state, you can move into spiritual healing mode with yourself or another person. Remember that you are working from a place of unconditional love so you remain unattached to any outcome. Spiritual healing works with the whole person, whether this is yourself or another whom you wish to help, and is not confined to addressing a specific condition. Have compassion for yourself, anyone else you may be working with, and for the condition itself.

Conscious breathing

Instead of letting it continue as an automatic process, conscious breathing is your decision to take temporary control of your breathing, as you have been doing during the earlier exercises, for example. Conscious breathing is also used to empower a person to play an active role in their healing, rather than remain a passive 'patient'. This brings feelings of safety and openness to healing.

EXERCISE 21

Initiation into the Healing Breath

Along with full-breath breathing, this breathing exercise reveals the power of the Breath of Unity to heal. The heart centre drives the breathing process and it is the open heart centre that creates the channel for healing energies to flow. Through the initiation into the Healing Breath, we receive practical evidence of the life

exercise continues ▶

force, or the divine presence, within the breath. The life force in the breath makes it possible to breathe in healing energies during any form of traditional or complementary therapy. Furthermore, this intention greatly enhances the effectiveness of those forms of healing.

The exercise is addressed to you, the self-healer, or the person who is to receive healing. You should either be sitting, or lying on your back on a couch or a clean surface on the ground.

Initiation into the Healing Breath prepares the energy field to receive healing energies. It may also be used to build upon your own body's potential to self-heal through relaxation. If you are working with a partner, he or she should talk you through the exercise, or you could record it, leaving pauses where necessary. If you are a healer, quietly and gently talk your patient through the exercise.

- Make yourself comfortable, relax and breathe normally. Close your eyes and focus on your breath and your breathing. Breathe in, breathe out.

- Feel your body breathing. Be aware of your breath entering and leaving your body. Enjoy the feeling of your body breathing. Feel your body moving in time with your breathing. Feel your chest and abdomen responding to your breathing.

- As you breathe in and breathe out, easily and gently, realise that this breath comes from a place where everything is safe, welcoming and loving.

- Imagine now that, as you inhale, you are taking in all the healing energy you need. And as you breathe out, your body is finding a way of letting go, releasing any stored energy you no longer need. Breathe in to nourish and heal yourself. Breathe out to let go of physical, mental and emotional problems.

- Feel yourself continually relaxing with every out-breath. Open yourself to the welcoming and loving space between each breath.

exercise continues ▶

- There is nothing else to do now but breathing and being, resting and receiving. There is nothing else to think about.

- Allow yourself to enjoy this realisation.

- Your body will continue to take in all the healing energy it needs and to release what it does not need on the out-breath. Spend a few moments in this healing state.

Because of its calming effect on the body, mind and emotions, this exercise usually leads to a deeply relaxed state. In a healing situation, the more calm and relaxed the person is, the more they are able to access the healing energy that is available. This happens because healing is the natural by-product of conscious union with the source of healing. A person's 'soft-belly' breathing signals that remembrance of unity with the Source has been established. At this point, it is common for a person to experience conscious union as a blissful state of non-separation and they may not want to return to everyday consciousness too quickly. Time should therefore be allowed for this.

When the exercise is carried out as a self-healing breathing activity, repeat the phrases above used by the 'healer'. If you are working with a partner, change roles and then compare notes together.

The exercise above effectively creates the energetic environment in which the person can experience their true spiritual nature. When this occurs, the realisation follows that all healing is a spiritual, rather than a physical, event. For this reason, a mechanistic way of healing that focuses solely on symptoms will never help a person to reconnect with their true, spiritual nature.

The power of the Healing Breath to reveal other aspects of the Source

The practice of combining conscious breathing and relaxation effectively closes our eyes to external stimuli and opens our brow centre, where inner vision is accessed. The next exercise goes further to engage your inner vision with your healing. Here, you will learn how to work with your energy field. In the context of the next exercise, Love, Peace and Light represent aspects of the Source. Some people find it helpful to see these three aspects of healing energy as colours. Love is often seen as a pink colour, Peace as blue, and Light as white. If you are working with someone else, your partner may see them all as different colours. Mentally record what colours you or your partner see because it may point to a specific healing need. For example, the colour yellow can indicate healing that is needed in the region of the solar plexus or a relevant organ. Other colours may relate to one or more of the other main energy centres (see the section on the seven main energy centres in Chapter 3, page 41).

EXERCISE 22

Using colour breathing to align with the energies of Love, Peace and Light

In this exercise, your breathing consciousness is extended as you use your brow centre to visualise the energies of Love, Peace and Light (as aspects of the Source) – the essential energies of healing – as colour vibrations. The exercise may also be used for self-healing. When combined with relaxation, the exercise is very suitable to begin any healing procedure. In addition, you are effectively putting yourself into a state of attunement with the Source, and choosing the vibration of healing energy that you need at this time (as demonstrated by the energy colours). You may experience different colours affecting specific body areas.

exercise continues ▶

Keep a record of this in your healing journal. If you are working with a partner, he or she should talk you through the exercise, or you could record it, leaving pauses where necessary.

- You should either be sitting on a chair with your feet flat on the floor, or comfortably on the ground, or lying on your back on a couch. Relax and breathe normally.

- Close your eyes. Pay attention to your breath and your breathing. Feel your body breathing and enjoy the movement of your body breathing.

- Some people describe the energy of healing as Love. Imagine that you can breathe in Love as the colour pink. As you exhale, surround yourself with this colour.

- Some describe the energy of healing as Peace. Imagine that you can breathe in Peace as the colour blue. As you exhale, surround yourself with this colour.

- Others people describe the energy of healing as Light. Imagine that you can breathe in Light as the colour white. As you exhale, surround yourself with this colour.

- Imagine your body filled and surrounded with the coloured energies of Love, Peace and Light.

- Rest in this state of alignment and attunement to the source of healing.

If you are working with a partner, change roles and talk your partner through the exercise. Compare notes together.

Visioning

Visualisation, as you discovered in the previous exercise, is about *imagining* what is there, creating it. Visioning, however, is a different process and should not be confused with visualisation. Visioning is the ability to see or sense what *is* actually there when you have this form of perception, or inner vision. Every one of us is born with a sense of our unique role in life. We do not imagine it for it is the truth about us. A person's reaction to life experiences may cloud this truth or put them out of touch with it completely. Sometimes ill-health, or a serious life problem, may be the catalyst that impels us to reconnect with or access the vision of who we are. To make that kind of connection is a form of visioning – of seeing what is actually there.

Visioning bypasses the conditioned mind of the personality so that the soul message of the vision is made available to us. The next exercise is designed to give you the opportunity to access a vision about a certain condition and to work towards healing it.

EXERCISE 23

Using the breath and inner visioning to help heal a condition

Spiritual healing works with the whole person and is not confined to addressing a specific condition, but it is always possible to use your ability to access an inner vision of a physical ailment or condition that you are experiencing. In this exercise, the creative facility of mind is brought into play to produce or receive a symbolic representation of the ailment or condition. This may range from a word or shape, to an actual picture. A symbol has the power to evoke information and feelings about a condition as well as simply describing it. Getting in touch with information and feelings about a condition may reinforce the healing process. Your vision of the symbol is thus a very empowering tool in self-healing or healing. The exercise may also be used as a self-healing activity to promote a relationship with a condition, which will make it easier for you to take action towards healing the condition.

If you are working with a partner, let him or her talk you through the exercise, or you could record it, leaving pauses where necessary.

exercise continues ▶

- Either sit on a chair with your feet flat on the floor or on the ground with your legs crossed. Alternatively, you could lie on your back on a couch. Relax and breathe normally.

- Close your eyes and focus on your breath and breathing. You are taking in all the energy you need at this time. Let go on the out-breath to release any stored energy you no longer need. Breathe in to nourish and heal yourself. Breathe out to let go of any physical, mental and emotional problems.

- Feel yourself becoming calmer and more relaxed with every out-breath.

- Without grasping at it, let a condition come to mind that you would like to work with. The condition can be physical, mental, or emotional. Let this condition be present to your awareness without directing any energy to it.

- If you experience the condition in your body, place your hands there. Notice if you feel compelled to put your hands any-where else on your body. Let your hands find where they want to rest. You are breathing into the etheric level of your energy field, which will receive the subtle healing energies of your breath.

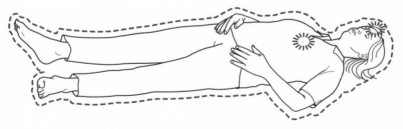

Figure 11: Using the breath and inner visioning to heal a condition

- Your breathing will show you if you can be present in a re-laxed way with this condition, with its pain or discomfort, and

exercise continues ▶

with any thoughts or feelings that may arise. Allow your breathing to help you stay calm and relaxed.

- Invite an image to come to mind that relates to the condition in some way. You may want to ask your higher self, 'What do I need to know?', or 'Show me what I need to see.'

- Staying calm and relaxed, allow the image to appear. It may take a few moments.

- Spend time with the image and try not to grasp at it. Remember your breathing. Be a detached observer, without needing to understand the image or to work it out at this stage.

- Notice the details about the image. Spend as long as feels comfortable with the image. It will signal when it is time to let go of it by gradually fading away.

- Without trying to hold on to the image, let it slip away. You can help this process with your out-breath.

- Give thanks and bring your attention back to your breath and your breathing. With every in-breath, allow yourself to gently return to a normal wakened state. With every out-breath, let go of the visioning.

- Through the process of allowing an image of a specific condition to come to mind, you are calmly making a relationship with the condition. This can be a great catalyst to initiate healing.

- Gradually become aware of your body. Use your breathing to help you connect fully with your physical body and your surroundings.

- Open your eyes and spend a few minutes relating to your surroundings.

- If you are working with a partner, discuss your experience with your partner when you feel ready. Work with your partner to interpret the image.

exercise continues ▶

- As a result of your experience, is there anything you need to do or say? Share this with your partner.

You may want to illustrate your image in your healing journal in order to record the healing experience and/or to continue working with the image and its unique message. The exercise may be practised once a day, ideally preceded by Exercises 20 and 21.

The energy exchange during healing

As sensitive people, we can learn how to control the flow of our energy out to others, so that we give our energy only when we want to. When you feel people drawing on your energy – as you will, by developing your sensitivity through conscious breathing and increased connection with the Source – check that you are breathing calmly and deeply. Offer up a prayer asking to be a channel for the energy that people need. In this way, energy can flow through you to be used by others, without your own reserves being depleted. Similarly, during self-healing you also ask to be the channel for your own healing.

The energies of vitality

Even though people will unconsciously draw on your energy in the normal course of events, you must not allow yourself to become depleted. When you feel your energy reserves are low, use one or more of the following set of exercises. The first allows you to access the raw energy of the planet. The next two allow you to access vitality energy. Vitality energy is processed by either the sacral energy centre or solar plexus energy centre. It comes to us from the physical and etheric levels of the Sun, and is essential to our well-being.

The orange vitality energy, which resonates most strongly with the sacral centre, energises and balances all the organs and systems of the sacral region, including the lower back. It is particularly useful for women. It nourishes the organs of reproduction and helps with menstrual problems and related conditions. The solar plexus centre's golden yellow vitality energy stimulates all the digestive organs in the region and the associated systems. It vitalises all other organs which may have become depleted and strengthens the etheric and other subtle bodies.

EXERCISE 24

Breathing in Earth energy

There may be times when you need the raw energies of the planet. These Earth energies are life-sustaining at a basic survival level and should be drawn in when your body has become run down.

- Take off your shoes and stand or sit comfortably with your feet flat on the ground.

- Regulate your breath until it is slow, gentle and rhythmic. As you breathe, visualise your feet making good contact with the ground. Enjoy this feeling of contact with the ground.

- Now breathe in, as if through the soles of the feet. Visualise the breath entering as energy through your feet.

- After three breaths, see the energy as a deep red, glowing light. With each in-breath, draw this energy up your legs and into the rest of your body. Keep breathing gently in this way until you feel fully energised. The red energy can be used to energise the pelvis and legs and to assist in balancing all conditions in these parts of the body.

See illustration on the page opposite.

exercise continues ▶

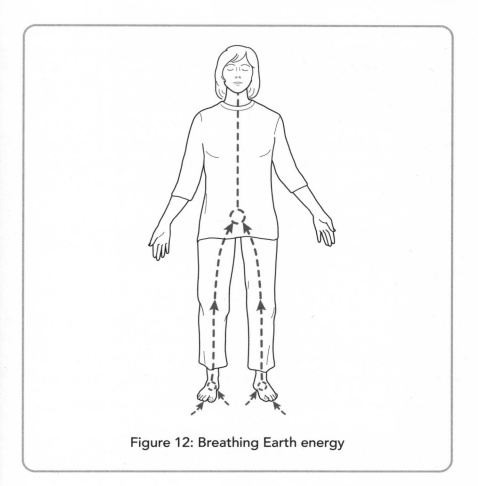

Figure 12: Breathing Earth energy

EXERCISE 25

Breathing in vitality energy – colour orange – to stimulate the sacral centre

The previous exercise may be followed by breathing in either or both of the two types of vitality energy present in the rays of the Sun. In this exercise, you imagine being able to breathe in the vitality energy needed by the sacral centre. This energy has the colour orange.

exercise continues ▶

- Stand or sit comfortably with your feet flat on the ground.

- Regulate your breath until it is slow, gentle and rhythmic. As you breathe, visualise your feet making good contact with the ground. Enjoy this feeling of contact with the ground.

- Focus on your sacral centre, just below your navel. Imagine that you can breathe a bright orange light into this centre. Now breathe this light into your sacral centre. Visualise the breath entering your sacral centre as energy.

- First allow the orange light to fill the energy centre and the whole sacral region. Then visualise the light flowing out into the rest of your body.

EXERCISE 26

Breathing in vitality energy – colour golden yellow – to stimulate the solar plexus centre

This vitality energy vibrates at a faster rate than orange vitality energy and so enters the etheric body through the solar plexus centre.

- Stand or sit comfortably with your feet flat on the ground.

- Breathe slowly, gently and rhythmically. As you breathe, visualise your feet making good contact with the ground. Enjoy this feeling of contact with the ground.

- Focus on your solar plexus centre, just below your ribcage. Imagine that you can breathe in this vitality energy as a golden yellow light.

- Allow the light to fill the centre and the whole solar plexus region. Then visualise golden yellow light flowing out into the rest of your body.

When you are in touch with your own energy levels, such as when you feel very tired or drained of energy, you can select any of the vitalising exercises to restore yourself at any particular time. Exercises 24–26 are particularly concerned with raising the energy levels of the physical body. The next exercise balances and revitalises the entire body and its energy systems, especially when working from the heart centre in any way. It is also an excellent antidote to the effects of negative energies on the centres.

EXERCISE 27

The energy centre revitalising breath

- Sit comfortably with your feet flat on the ground. Rest your hands on your thighs, palms up. Breathe normally.

- Relax your elbows, the back of your neck and the tops of your shoulders. Do this by letting go of any tension with each out-breath. Close your eyes if this helps you concentrate.

- First, breathe into your heart centre. As you slowly inhale, visualise a green light in your heart centre that gets brighter each time you inhale. As you inhale, allow the green light to fill up your heart centre and move out to the area of your body around it.

- Let your focus move slowly and gently down to your solar plexus centre, just below the ribcage. As you inhale visualise a golden yellow light and allow this light to fill up the centre and the area around it.

- Now let your focus move down to your sacral centre, just below your navel. As you inhale visualise a bright orange light; allow this light to fill up the centre and spill out to the area around it.

- Let your focus move slowly and gently down to your base centre, at the base of your spine. Inhale and visualise a bright

exercise continues ▶

red light. Allow this light to fill up the centre and the area around it.

- Return your focus to your heart centre. See the green light awaiting you. Let your focus gently rise to your throat centre. As you inhale visualise a sky-blue light and allow this light to fill up the centre and the areas of your throat, nose and ears.

- Let your focus gently rise to your brow centre, just above the middle of your forehead. Inhale and visualise a royal blue or indigo light. Allow this light to fill up the centre and your head and eyes.

- Let your focus slowly and gently rise at last to your crown centre, at the top of your head. As you inhale visualise a violet light. Allow this light to fill up the centre, and cover the top of your head.

- Return your focus to your heart centre. See the green light awaiting you again. Relax and breathe naturally.

Thought, colour and the breath

Recalling how energy follows thought and how thought and mindsets follow your breathing, here are two simple exercises which combine thought, visualisation and breathing to create positive effects. You can practise them whenever you need to without sitting down or standing still.

EXERCISE 28

Thinking pink, breathing pink

Deep pink is the colour of unconditional love energy. It has profound healing effects and you can always surround yourself, a person, or a situation with this energy by 'thinking pink'. The

exercise continues ▶

nervous system is soothed and the etheric body strengthened by pink energy. Pink energy also has the power to change attitudes and thinking patterns from negative to positive and gives powerful help to anything that is bruised, torn or injured, whether this is a person or a situation.

- Become aware of your breathing and, if the subject is another person, become aware of this other person's breathing rhythm.

- Imagine that you can send a bright pink light out to a person, or a situation, as the case may be.

- Breathe in. As you exhale, visualise a sphere of pink light around the subject. Coordinate the visualisation with your breathing and send this pink energy on the out-breath. If it is difficult for you to see colour, visualise something pink like a bunch of pink roses or a pink balloon.

If you are going to a difficult meeting or an interview, project pink into the room beforehand. This will not of course make the meeting go *your* way, and you won't get the job if it is not right for you, but it will encourage an outcome which is best for all the parties concerned. It will also help create a relaxed atmosphere of trust and confidence. If you feel you need it, you can always surround yourself with this energy colour, as described in the exercise above.

EXERCISE 29

Thinking green, breathing green

It is no coincidence that people go off to the country when they need to find peace and balance. The green colours of the plant world supply these valuable vibrations. Breathe them in and always give thanks to the plant world for their gift. Use this exercise whenever you feel out of balance emotionally or mentally,

exercise continues ▶

such as when you feel upset. As with 'thinking pink', you can always surround yourself, a person or situation with the energies of balance and calm by thinking bright green. This energy also changes attitudes, impulses and thinking patterns from negative to positive. It gives powerful help to anyone or anything that is out of balance or in need of calming down.

- Become aware of your breathing. As you breathe in, visualise a bright green light being drawn down to the crown of your head. As you continue to breathe in, this colour flows down over your head and body, and then flows out to fill your energy field.

- With your in-breath, hold the thought: 'I breathe in peace and balance.' On the out-breath release the cause of your tension or upset state.

- Now breathe the green light in through your crown centre and let it fill your body. Again, breathe with the thought: 'I breathe in peace and balance.'

The energy of green light may also be used to energise the organs in the chest, the heart and circulatory system. Breathe the green light into the heart centre. Allow it to fill the heart centre and then the physical body via the heart centre's etheric channels and the thymus gland under the top of the breastbone. The lungs and bronchial tubes also benefit from this energy.

- To activate the second aspect of this exercise, become aware of your breathing and, if the subject is a person, become aware of this person's breathing rhythm.

- Imagine that you can send a bright green light out to a person, or a situation, as the case may be.

- Breathe in. As you exhale, visualise a sphere of green light around the subject. Coordinate the visualisation with your breathing and send this energy on the out-breath. Try to visualise something that is green like grass or the leaves on a tree, if you have problems seeing colours.

Your heart centre

Your heart centre is the meeting point, and the place of balance, between your physical life and your spiritual life. Deep contact with your heart centre enables you to have access to both these worlds, while, at the same time, giving you access to the world of your higher self and its mission. Many of the exercises in this book emphasise this dimension of your heart centre, and how breathing is the way in to the centre. But all the issues about love in your life – how you love, who you love, who loves you, perhaps a lack of love – will affect your breathing and your connection with your higher self. This is why it is important to review the state of your heart centre from time to time. For example, you can find valuable insights by looking into your heart centre to assess whether or not you are equipped to be wholehearted in what you say and do.

The crucial role of the out-breath in healing

A person's out-breath creates an unobstructed pathway for incoming healing energy because the out-breath clears energetic debris. This release of energetic debris is made possible by the blood, which carries the energies of the etheric body, the endocrine glands, the nervous system, and the life force, as well as dissolved gases. Although the lungs are involved in expelling waste gases via the out-breath, they do not deal with the subtle energy stream involved with healing. During a healing session, as the energy of the out-breath is moving down through the body, the body presents energy to this outgoing stream to be discharged. The process begins on the physical level, followed by the emotional and then the mental levels.

On a subtle energetic level, energetic discharge takes place with a wave-like motion, in time with the rhythm of each out-breath, as it moves down the central channel of the subtle body until it reaches the feet (via the base energy centre and its link with the sole-of-the-foot centres). Thus, the discharged subtle energies involved in healing leave the body via either the base or the sole-of-the-foot energy centres.

The next exercise illustrates this healing role of the out-breath. By using your imagination, you are able to cooperate with, and experience, the energetic process of the out-breath, as outlined above.

EXERCISE 30

A breathing detox

- Lie down in a comfortable place. Close your eyes. Allow your mind to rest on your breath. Become aware of your body breathing.

- Place a little more emphasis on your out-breath. As you exhale, imagine that you can send the energy of the out-breath down your body and visualise it leaving your body via the soles of your feet.

- Continue 'emptying' yourself this way with each out-breath. Your in-breath will bring new healthy energy to replace the discharged energies. You can conclude the discharge breath when you feel emptied of energetic debris, renewed, or refreshed.

Breath and the journeying soul

Moment by moment, your breath reminds you that your higher self is always journeying with you and that your soul is always present in your heart centre. Similarly, the healer is always journeying with the patient, bearing witness to the patient's experience of life throughout the healing process and joining this through joining with the patient's breathing. Your breath and your heart will tell you that self-healing depends on your developing a relationship with your present condition at any given time. Your condition is the soul's best way of describing the current inner state of being, within the context of the life journey. The pattern of your breathing bears witness to your state of being.

If you are a healer, you will need to understand that every condition or problem that a person has is what they have chosen as their path towards integration with their higher self. Even confusion should be welcomed as a situation in which a person is seeking an understanding of the personality, the higher self, and their relationship to each other. With your awareness of the breath and your focus in the heart centre, you do not fear a condition, its name, or your experience of it, so you do not need to have power over it.

A crisis is an opportunity to work and grow with the mission of soul, and an opportunity to be open to the healing energies that are accessed via the breath. In this way you come to recognise and welcome the creative function of any condition that you want to work with, and its role in your life journey. With this attitude, you can be present to yourself, without judgement or expectations. The function of healing is not to take something away before you have had the chance to gain insight into your condition. Your breath and your heart will tell you to wait upon the divine within you, and to enter that place of light where soul can come through and take the leading role in your life, and breathe.

Chapter 8

Your breathing day

With the rising of the morning sun, your new day comes into being. In the traditions of many Native American tribes, this is seen as a sacred moment. For example, Tecumseh, Chief of the Shawnee (c.1768–1813), saw this time as an opportunity for celebration and thanksgiving – for the morning light, for life and strength, for food and for the sheer joy of living. In this chapter, we will take a look at breathing practices that will help you to more fully engage with each and every day, to embrace the adventures that this human life presents and to remember sacred unity. Just as your breathing has a certain rhythm, so every day has its own rhythm. When we are aligned with any rhythm, we are in balance with it. As you have discovered so far, being in balance is another facet of self-healing.

EXERCISE 31

Greeting the day

When you greet the new day, you open yourself to the energies of the Source. As you will recall if you have ever watched someone asleep, night-time and daytime breathing rhythms are different.

exercise continues ▶

By gently aligning your breathing rhythm to the rhythms of the new day, this exercise awakens all your systems to the new cycle brought by daylight.

Practise the exercise outside when you can, but it is perfectly all right to practise it indoors too. Here, seven breaths of greeting are sent out to the seven directions of East, South, West, North, Above, Below and Within. At the beginning of a new day, you take in the energy of each of the seven directions.

- Either standing or sitting, face the direction of the dawn, the place of the rising sun (East). Use your breath to relax your body. Become aware of your feet and their contact with the ground. Feel your connection to the Earth.

- Give thanks for the previous night. Be aware that the Source of energy, and the promise of each day, is within you.

- Feel the air around you. Become aware of your breath and the fresh air entering your nostrils and your lungs. Note how your whole body enjoys the breath of the new day.

- As you breathe slowly and naturally, raise your arms above your head, as if lifting them up to the Sun.

- In this position of thanks and greeting, inhale and visualise the life force in the air moving into your physical body and your energy field.

- With your next breath, breathe in the energies of direction East. Exhale.

- Turn 'sunwise' (clockwise), to face the South. Breathe in the energies of direction South. Exhale.

- Turn sunwise, to face the West. Breathe in the energies of direction West. Exhale.

- Turn sunwise, to face the North. Breathe in the energies of direction North. Exhale.

exercise continues ▶

- Turn sunwise once more, to face the East. Raising your head to acknowledge the sky, breathe in the energies of direction Above. Exhale.

- Bowing your head to acknowledge the Earth, breathe in the energies of direction Below. Exhale.

- Lower your arms and cross them over your heart centre. Breathe in and acknowledge the energies of direction Within. Exhale.

- Enjoy this state of harmony for a few moments before resuming your everyday activities.

If you are able to practise the exercise outside, notice the world around you as you calmly take your breaths. Feel the renewal of your sacred connection with life. Acknowledge the other life forms that may be present.

The subtle aspects of food

Living things need nourishment, and greeting the day helps prepare us for the first meal of the day. The digestive system, like all the other bodily systems, works at a subtle as well as a physical level with the food and drink we consume. The physical function of digestion begins in the mouth, as does the subtle level of digestion. The finest energy vibrations of the food are absorbed by the tongue. These vibrations then interact with the life force. The body needs the subtle aspects of food and drink and will find ways of alerting us if it does not get enough in quality and quantity.

Because food has been part of a living plant or animal, it contains a range of energy vibrations, including the vibrations that have been absorbed during processing. Blessing your meals expresses gratitude towards your food and clears your food of unwanted energies, if this is needed (and it often is). A food blessing can also bring the food's energies into alignment with your own. In the next exercise, the breath is central to creating the alignment between you and your food.

Offering a blessing ensures that all food can be honoured through your remembrance of the subtle link between your heart centre and the centres of your palms, described on page 57. This link is expressed via the breath when you visualise breathing into the heart centre and exhaling through your palms. The second aspect of blessing is that gratitude for your food may be expressed by vocalising the heart's message via the breath. Start your day by blessing your breakfast.

EXERCISE 32

Blessing your food

- Before you begin eating, first hold your hands over the food to see if your body really needs it.

- If you sense that it does not, listen to your intuitive awareness and do not consume the food. This will probably not be the case with your first meal of the day.

- With your hands held either over your meal or in a gesture of thanksgiving and blessing, take a full breath. As you breathe out, use your voice to bless and thank the food and drink.

- You may also want to thank those who prepared it for you, or who brought it to your table.

Your spontaneous words, or even a sacred verse or syllable, may be more valid than something said by rote on a regular basis without awareness. The effect of a blessing and a thanksgiving is always positive and beneficial for others who are eating with you.

Blessing your food particularly affects its subtle aspects. The subtle energies of your breath link with the subtle energies of your food. A breathing blessing is able to breathe life back into depleted food, especially that which has undergone industrial processing. Food should always be eaten with enjoyment and never with anxiety about what it is made of or where it has come from. Blessing your food can alleviate this anxiety, so go ahead and enjoy your food as a gift from the planet and the Source. When circumstances prevent you from giving thanks-giving and blessing your food out loud, do it mentally. This can be especially beneficial when eating out, when you don't know where the food has come from or how it has been prepared.

Having an open mind

You will benefit by being able to approach your day with an open mind. This enables you to accept and be positively aware of what the new day has to offer. Opening the mind is a physiological, as well as mental, process, because the mind and body are interconnected. They are both part of the total vehicle that our soul has created in order to express itself on Earth. You may recall that thought and action are linked by the breath and breathing. The first step in guiding the mind begins with conscious breathing to calm and balance it.

EXERCISE 33

Breathing to open your mind

Practise this exercise at the beginning of the day, or before you begin any mental or creative work.

- Sit or lie down comfortably and quietly, breathing in the life that is all around you. Allow your breathing rhythm to move in harmony with how you sense the rhythm of this life.

- As you inhale into your abdomen, feel yourself taking in the energy of life. Do you sense this as light, and, if so, does it have a colour? If you sense the life energy as a dull colour at first, com-bine each breath with your imagination to visualise it as a more energising, bright colour. Repeat the process six or seven times.

- Next, imagine that you can take in the energy of life through your crown centre. As you pause and then exhale, sense this

exercise continues ▶

energy flowing through your body and exiting via the sole-of-the-foot centres. Do you sense this energy as light, and, if so, does it have a colour? Again, if you sense the life energy as a dull colour at first, combine each breath with your imagination to visualise it as a bright colour. Do this six or seven times while watching the energy flow into, through and out of your body with the rhythm of your breath.

- Now imagine that, as you take the energy of life into your crown centre, it completely fills your brain. Pause, and then as you exhale, feel your brain expand as it is nourished by the life force. Repeat the process six or seven times.

- You may feel a little light-headed by the end of this exercise. Stay in your sitting or reclining position until your sensations return to normal. Focus your attention on your hands and feet. Wiggle your fingers and toes. Return completely to your body before you get up or resume your work.

The creative person within

We are each gifted with the responsibility of creating our day. The open mind tells us that, no matter what tasks we have to do, the mind–breath link is always available to us to make our days, our work and our relationships sacred.

Every moment in the life of every person, and every being, is a moment of creation because the divine within gives us the potential to be co-creator with the Source. If you observe any part of the natural world for even a short time, you will be struck by the unceasing process of creation. Creation is part of life. You are part of life, and you are just as able to be creative.

With your mind open to this potential, and to suggestions you may receive from your higher self, you can celebrate the creative person within you, who has been there since your first breath. Being creative is not about being skilled or expert at something, it is about allowing the divine within (which is the artist within) to simply do what it needs to do, without fear or judgement. Being creative is an opportunity to release the unique, essential you into your life and into the world.

Any kind of creative act is a form of healing. It is a way to address any sense of separation from other beings, the universe, even the Source. When you call forth the artist within, you recall your Oneness with all that is, and you reconnect with creation. Being creative is as natural as your breathing. Breathe in what you want to create, and, with your out-breath, allow it to form itself. With the next exercise, you can help open up these possibilities for yourself.

EXERCISE 34

Breathing to release your creativity

- Stand or sit where you wish to do some creative work. Use your breathing to relax your body. Breathe normally.

- Bring your attention to your sacral centre below your navel, the centre that processes all issues of creativity. See it glowing as a 'ball' of orange light. Imagine this light summoning up more and more of your creativity.

- Now visualise the subtle connection between your sacral and throat centres as a thread of light linking them together. Recall that your throat centre processes all issues to do with communication and expression, especially the expression of the authentic you and your creative faculty.

- As you inhale, draw up the 'ball' of creative energy and move it from your sacral centre to your throat centre via the thread of light that connects them.

- As it passes through the solar plexus region, your ball of creative energy absorbs the input of the wisdom and guidance of intelligence and reason. As it passes through the heart centre, it facilitates the input of the wisdom and guidance of unconditional love.

exercise continues ▶

- Once the ball of creative energy reaches your throat, breathe out. On this out-breath, visualise your creative energy settling comfortably in your throat.

- With the next breath, focus on your brow centre. As you exhale, visualise the energy of the brow centre streaming down to the throat as a royal blue or indigo light. This sends the wisdom and guidance of intuition to combine with your ball of creative energy.

- With your next breath, focus on your crown centre. As you exhale, visualise violet or bright purple light streaming down to your throat centre, combining with the ball of creative energy and giving you access to spiritual direction.

Practise the complete exercise, noting what feels comfortable or uncomfortable. By placing your attention in your heart centre and keeping it there for a minute or so, you might be able to uncover why you are feeling this comfort or discomfort. Later, as you decide on a creative task, use the parts of the exercise that you intuitively feel will help you. Keep a note of your findings in your healing journal. A pattern may appear that shows how you involve specific energy centres according to the task in hand.

The Breath of Connection

Creative moments occur when we no longer worry about our sense of self or ego or what it wants. This is because the creative energy with which we make connection has its origins outside of self. The creative connection joins us with our higher self so that inspiration (like the intake of vital breath) floods in. Time very often passes quickly or may seem to stand still in these creative moments. The creative connection that breathing links us with is like the sharing of a lover's kiss.

As we grow up, we intuitively realise that there is something special about kissing, and we wonder about our first 'real' kiss. We may not be aware that it is the sharing of the breath of life with someone that makes kissing so special. With someone we love, the shared mouth-to-mouth kiss teaches us about union and the flow of life. The experience of union, through a lover's kiss, may take us to a dimension where we find out about sacred breath and creation. The mutual giving and receiving in the mouth-to-mouth kiss is the true breath of connection. The breath as true connection is the meaning behind the Hawaiian greeting 'Aloha', where alo implies sharing and ha is the breath, or essence, of life. 'Aloha' thus acknowledges and reminds us that we share the breath of life with one another.

Being present and making connections

In your relations and interactions with others, how much of you is in your breath? Too much, not enough, or are you breathing out to others in a way that encourages them to breathe back to you? At some point in your practise of the exercises so far, you may have noticed to what extent you have been present and connected with yourself. If you have been fortunate enough to practise some of the exercises with a partner or in a group situation, you will have needed to connect with them, to be present to them.

Whether you knew it or not, when this connection was being made, it was facilitated by your breath. When you breathe to connect with a person, an animal, a plant, a landscape, or a situation, this is your way to be totally present to them. The breath, then, is the key to directing your energy so that it flows and energetically links you to others. Energy follows thought and, with practise, your thinking will follow your breath. Your breath allows you to be totally present and to communicate this state of engaged awareness.

Presence is essential to living life consciously, to expressing yourself, to using your talents and creativity, and to having meaningful relationships with others and your surroundings. Making the full breath a natural, everyday way of breathing is a valuable tool in helping you to be present to life, rather than being virtually unconscious of it.

Though there are ways of breathing that can ensure your connection with life, some breaths lack the vitality or will to connect, and still others are intended to dominate or dismiss, rather than connect. The breath that will never link our presence with another does not have the energy to do so. This is because of poor intentions due to a lack of self-worth, fear, lack of confidence, distrust and so on. The breath that seeks to dominate or dismiss others may have similar origins, but it is delivered with an aggressive force that has no intention of connecting with others.

Many of our relationships, however brief, have suffered from lack of connection because there was little attempt to be present. The Breath of Connection becomes a potent self-healing tool in ensuring that we will be present to others. The breath that connects with others is delivered with the intention of mutual engagement. This breath allows others to reciprocate, thus creating the breathing cycle of connection. The way to deal with those who fail to connect with you, or those who seek to intimidate or overlook you, is to use your breath to connect with them. This creates the opportunity for real dialogue and real relationship, and it can be applied to every situation.

The work of voice and acting coaches, such as Patsy Rodenburg, has shown that the Breath of Connection is the essential tool for an actor or any kind of public speaker to effectively communicate with their audience. This next breathing exercise ensures that you communicate *with*, rather than talk *at*, your audience. It is about interaction with another, or other, living beings. The exercise shows you how the connecting breath feels and how to use it.

EXERCISE 35

The Breath of Connection

The breath contains three primordial elements of creation: Fire, Water and Air. We will use these properties of the breath to begin our investigation into how it may be used to facilitate connection. This exercise can be practised indoors or outside. Find a place without too many distractions, and, since you will want to feel your breath as it touches your hand, avoid practising outside if it is a windy day.

exercise continues

- Stand or sit comfortably and breathe naturally, through your nose, if possible. Relax your body. Become aware of your natural breathing rhythm.

- Hold one hand up in front of your face, about a foot away. Look at your hand. Breathe in. Exhale with the intention to touch your hand with your breath.

- Be aware of the sound of your breath and its movement. Be aware of your breath as it touches your hand. Sense its warmth and moistness.

- Still holding your hand in front of your face, look at your hand and breathe in. Breathe out halfway towards your hand. Notice how you feel. What happened to your breath? This breath is too stunted to make connection with your hand.

- Look at your hand again and breathe in. This time, as you exhale, breathe towards a place beyond or well to the side of your hand. Notice how you feel. What happened to your breath? This breath is too misdirected to make connection with your hand.

- Lower your hand and check that your body is relaxed. Use your breath to make connections to other parts of the room or your surroundings. Each time, focus on your target as you breathe in (your target may be at any distance from you). Breathe out with the intention to connect with the target. Notice how you breathe. Notice how the connections feel.

- Now make a connection in the same way by breathing out to another person. Notice how you breathe. Notice how the connections feel.

Connecting with another person is about sharing the life force, even if those concerned are not aware of this. The Breath of Connection makes its most important connections at a subtle level, beginning with the etheric.

Breath as a weapon or as a means of defence

When we use our hands as a means to hurt another being, it is relayed to the heart centre as negative energy. The heart centre does its best to process this information, but, when there is an energetic overload of negativity, it may cope by closing down its processing. In the long-term, this will lead to an inability to access heart qualities such as compassion or loving kindness – the opposite of self-healing.

We can also use our voice as a destructive weapon by speaking in a harmful way, or using words that are abusive, humiliating, or love-less. Again, these energies will have a harmful effect on their target, but they will also harm the speaker. The sacral, heart, throat and brow energy centres are all involved in processing the activities of the voice and the breathing that enables the voice.

However, there is another more positive side to using breath as a personal weapon or tool. We can utilise our breath, our voice and the power of our lower three energy centres – the base, sacral and solar plexus centres – to protect our personal boundaries and to defend our-selves. When you do not want something to happen, you have to be able to say 'No' in the way that is most appropriate to the situation. Saying 'No' asserts your equality and dignity as a human being.

EXERCISE 36

Saying 'No'

When you don't want something in life, you are perfectly entitled to say 'No', yet some people struggle to do this for a variety of reasons. They might feel disempowered, or they fear it might seem to the person asking like a rejection, ingratitude, or rude-ness. Such reasons are excuses for not asserting our right to be. To get used to using this exercise in a real-life situation, first practise by visualising a situation where you would need to use it.

- To say no effectively, first make visual contact with the other person. Direct your out-breath to the other person.

exercise continues ▶

- Move your mind from your solar plexus centre to your heart centre. Continue sending your out-breath to the other person.

- Breathe out your 'No'. It does not have to overpower the person or come from a place of fear or panic. When spoken kindly, but firmly, the energy of your 'No' is saying: 'I do not want that and it is no reflection on you.'

Pay attention to your breathing throughout the exercise. Good breathing keeps us centred. When we are centred people are more able to hear and sense our 'No'. 'No' is a very powerful word when uttered with conviction. So are words like 'Stop!' In the next exercise, your right to say 'No' is extended to perform a more defensive role.

EXERCISE 37

Saying 'No' to defend yourself

When you are in a situation that is threatening, you have the right to reject the situation. When the threat comes in the form of one or more persons, your defiant rejection of the threat could be life-saving.

First decide where the energy of your power is stored. For women, this is often in the sacral centre, the place of the womb. For men, it is often in the base centre. The solar plexus is a great reservoir of power, too, but we have to know how to access it. To get used to using this exercise in a real-life situation first practise by visualising a situation where you would need to use it. You will soon locate the centre that delivers your defiant shout with the most conviction. Having used your breath to calm yourself, deliver your 'No!' from your place of power.

You will need to experiment. If your solar plexus is over-whelmed by thoughts of fear and panic, you will have to use

exercise continues ▶

your breath to calm yourself. If your base centre is pumping adrenaline and other survival hormones into your bloodstream, you can utilise this when you say 'No' to defend yourself.

- Use your breath to bring calm so that your flight-or-fight reactions are in your favour.

- Practise attuning yourself to whichever centre your defensive power is in.

- Breathe deeply into this centre. Gather your power and exhale from this centre, joining your breath with the shout 'No!'

- Use your breathing to link with the people concerned and breathe out to them, but be ready to send them an overpowering message.

Breath as affirmation

We live in a world of polarity where everything has two sides. The voice and the breath can be used in very destructive ways, and we need to know how to recognise and counteract these ways when we come across them. However, your voice can be used in a positive way to defend and affirm your right to be. It can also be used to send creative and vitalising energies out to the world. We all need the voice of support and validation, the voice of generosity and forgiveness, the loving and caring voice.

Once you have practised breathing into and out from your heart centre, you will find it progressively easier to use your voice as a means to create well-being for yourself and others. The energy of this way of breathing and speaking lends a positive pitch and tone to your voice. Its effect will always be positive and life-affirming.

EXERCISE 38

The Supportive Voice

- Focus on your heart centre. Breathe into and out of your heart centre for a few breaths.

- Form a picture in your mind's eye of someone who needs support.

- Now choose a phrase from the list below and breathe it out to the person in your mind's eye. For example, as you exhale from your heart centre, you could say:

  I love you...

  I'll support you...

  You can depend on me...

- As you exhale, repeat your chosen phrase for as many times as you wish.

Add more phrases of your own to practise your supportive voice. When you want to say something positive with conviction, breathe what you want to say to another from your heart centre. Each one of us has a voice. Use your voice and the power of your breath to share your visions and your viewpoints with others and the world.

Sacred presence

Indigenous spirituality, such as the Native American or that of the Australian Aboriginals, asserts that there is a sacred presence in all things – in animals, flowers, trees, rocks – as well as in human beings. When we are aware of the sacred presence (or the divine within) in anyone or any thing, we are truly present to that person, being, or thing.

From now on, practise your awareness of the sacred presence. Use your breath to make connections with your workplace, shopping places, places of leisure, your landscape, or your cityscape. Breathe to make connections with other people: the person at the checkout counter, strangers, friends, colleagues, your partner, your lover. Notice how they all react positively to your breath of connection. Yes, this does apply to your pet and other animals, your pot plant and other members of the plant world, your crystal, the ground, and the whole of the mineral kingdom! It is always our *disconnections* that call for self-healing.

Because all matter comes from the source of consciousness, everything is conscious at some level. Acknowledging this, you could also seek sacred presence in and make breathing connection with your car, your computer, the tools you work or cook with, and so on. In this way, conscious connection to life, through the breath of life, becomes a step-by-step way to discovering who you really are.

A good walk is ideal for contemplating these thoughts in a relaxed way. It will take you outside and into the fresh air, where you can find an appreciation of your breathing.

Ending the day well

Before you prepare for bed, you need to have a routine that enables you to let go of the day's activities. This should be done at least an hour before sleep. Take some moments to assess your day in a detached frame of mind. Tell yourself that you are going to look back over the day, not to praise or blame but to see what has been achieved, no matter how small that achievement may be.

EXERCISE 39

Reviewing your day

- Sit or lie down comfortably. Breathe normally and relax your body.

- Think back to the morning. What was your mood like? What did you set out to achieve and did you achieve it? How did

exercise continues ▶

you react to things that happened or problems that occurred? As you recall these situations, what is happening to your breathing? If necessary, take steps to return it to your normal rhythm.

- How did you react to the good things in your day?

- Did you remember your breathing at crucial moments?

- Now decide how you might react if these crucial moments in your day happened again.

- Many people may have crossed your path today. Did anyone stand out for any particular reason? Did anyone need your help?

- How have you reacted to these people? Did you remember to breathe towards them in order to make a connection? As you recall these situations, what is happening to your breathing? If necessary, take steps to return it to your normal rhythm. This involves letting go of any people and/or situations on the out-breath.

- You are developing an awareness of yourself and others as beings of light. Did you see the light of another person today? Were you really looking for it?

- Having considered all these aspects of your day, as if you are a detached observer, simply let them go. The things of tomorrow will be dealt with tomorrow by the new you.

Preparing for sleep

A routine of meditation and/or prayer will create a calm, purposeful atmosphere around you, and the right frame of mind for sound sleep and useful dreaming. Your next day really begins the night before. This is because your final thoughts and feelings on any given day will affect the quality of your sleep and the day which follows. The thoughts and feelings from the day before are the energy base you will have to build on during the following day.

Before retiring to bed, check that you will be as physically comfortable as possible. You will not sleep well if you are still digesting a big meal. You will not sleep well if you have given your mind too much to digest. Do you really want troublesome news images stored in your mind, let alone last thing at night? Physical, emotional and mental indigestion mean that your valuable dream time will be taken up on the etheric level with processing the agitation this causes in your psyche.

Check that your mind and emotions are calm, and do not attempt to sleep with an unresolved argument or harsh words ringing in your ears. An apology or other peaceful overture, as appropriate, could be a small price to pay for an untroubled mind and a good night's sleep. Emotional and mental turmoil ruins sleep. If you cannot sleep because of your disturbed thoughts, you are under stress. Waking in the night or the following morning with the same troubled thoughts on your mind as the day before is a sure sign of stress. Before it becomes a source of serious energy loss and imbalance, address the cause by using the relevant breathing exercises from Chapter 5.

EXERCISE 40

Preparing for sleep

Check that your body is still relaxed, as in Exercise 39: Reviewing your day. Give thanks for your day. You have done what you can. Before going to sleep, prepare to 'travel light' into your dream time by carrying out any of the relevant constructive actions necessary mentioned above.

- If you need to clear your subtle energy systems of negative media images and stories, use your out-breath to release them. If you have practised anything that will open your energy centres beyond their everyday functioning (such as an energising breathing exercise or reading about a spiritual subject),

exercise continues ▶

carry out Exercise 5: The Closing-down Procedure (page 47). The silver energy in the first part of this exercise will reinforce any necessary clearing function.

- If you carry out distant healing and wish to be a channel for healing during the hours of sleep, tell yourself that this will be on condition that you will not awake feeling depleted of energy.

- You are ready to look forward to your sleep. If you have taken all the precautions described above, any remaining difficulties in going to sleep generally stem from thinking. This means that you are situated in your solar plexus centre – the place where thoughts and emotions are processed.

- Make a conscious effort to move out of this centre into the one above it – your heart centre. Put your mind there and become aware of your breath. This is the Breath of Unity: your moment-by-moment connection with the Source or your higher self within.

- Put yourself in the care of your higher self and allow yourself to relax and drift into sleep. You may not be able to achieve this first time. As soon as you find yourself thinking, move your consciousness back into your heart centre. With practice you will find that the move into your heart centre becomes routine.

Once you find that Exercise 40 (Preparing for sleep) is helping you, you are ready to have a more conscious relationship with your dreams.

Dreams

It is a natural and healthy aspect of sleep to dream. Once you move into deep sleep your consciousness moves out of your body and links with your higher self. During the day, you can listen to the voice of your higher self in your heart centre and receive that level of guidance from your brow centre. During sleep, dreams help us to do two important things that we may not have done, for whatever reason, during the waking state. These are sorting images and information received during the day, and having communion with our soul or higher self. This second function forms the basis of the dream-related breathing exercise that follows.

The dream as a self-healing tool and part of traditional medicine can be traced back beyond two millennia to the healing centres of Asklepios (the god of medicine and healing) in ancient Greece. People needing help, ranging from the physical and psychological to the spiritual, would be encouraged to enter the dream state to make contact with the divine physician within – the higher self. Most cultures have revered and respected the function of the dream state and its ability to bypass the mind and its conditioning to give us access to the wisdom of the higher self. It has also become an integral part of many disciplines, such as psychology, and an integral part of many therapies, such as psychotherapy.

If we understand that dream material is presented by the higher self for use by the personality, we can understand its language. Just as the higher self 'speaks' to us during our waking state through the medium of feelings, so it uses exactly the same 'language' in the dream state: the language of feelings. Even images are presented as symbolic of feelings or they generate certain feelings within us. You can recognise any dream coming from the level of the higher self by these qualities: it is vivid, it is in colour and it makes you *feel* something during and after the dream.

Feeling is the key to dreams

The dream is first and foremost a profound soul experience and a necessary aspect of our link with the soul. The dream may be there to help, but it is your *soul* material – don't expect the mind to understand it. Trying to interpret your dream is generally a task to satisfy the ego, as is using other people's interpretations or books of so-called dream symbols. The key to dreams lies less in understanding and far more in making a connection with your feelings (the language of the soul) and, in so doing, making connection with your higher self and perhaps its message of wisdom and helpful guidance. This is the base line of the exercise that follows.

EXERCISE 41

Preparing to dream

This exercise follows on immediately and naturally from Exercise 40: Preparing for sleep.

- If you wish to remember your dreams, tell yourself that you will do this but that you will not try to force the situation.

- Make a decision to observe the pictures and images that appear to your inner vision rather than follow the endless trail of thoughts that your mind presents you with. Remember that, as with so many of the breathing exercises for self-healing, you are making a connection with your higher self.

- You can facilitate this by moving your consciousness to your brow centre. Become aware of your breathing. Allow yourself to breathe into this centre and to breathe out from it.

- Recall that you are breathing the Breath of Unity: your moment-by-moment connection with the Source or your higher self within.

- Put yourself in the care of your higher self and allow yourself to relax and drift into sleep.

- When you awake from a dream, whatever the time of night or day, ask yourself, 'How do I feel?' Dreams have pictures about feelings. You need to get in touch with your feelings first and recalling the dream images may help you to recall the feelings of the dream. Here again you need to make a connection. It will help you to connect with your dreams if you imagine that you can breathe towards, or back into, them.

- Later, if you can, try talking with another person about your dream and how you felt while you were asleep. Explain to them that you need their support and listening ear rather than their interpretations.

exercise continues ▶

- Finally, you may need to take some action based on your connection with your dream feelings and/or your dream wisdom. Consciously filter your plan of action through your heart centre, rather than your conditioned mind (through the solar plexus centre).

The last three exercises, around ending your day well, will help to balance your experience of the day and the night, as well as the human and the spiritual. By making the exercises an integral part of your self-healing programme you will bring health to all levels of your being. Aim to go slowly towards your goal so that you can enjoy the experience. Sleep well, dream well!

Chapter 9

The breathing voice: vocalising the sacred

In the beginning was sound

In his book *The Mozart Effect*, musician, teacher and healer Don Campbell asserts that everyone, though they may not admit it, loves singing or chanting. This simple and natural use of our voice has great self-healing potential, as the work of many like Don Campbell will testify. At the age of four, in a kindergarten run by an elderly lady, I experienced the joy of singing with others. We had to sit up straight, breathe into our 'tummy' and sing with gusto. Our wonderful teacher would lift her hands and look expectantly at each of us; it was our cue to breathe in. Her look told us that we had more than enough energy to sing. As her arms danced and her eyes widened, out of our mouths would come rousing folk songs, some of which I can still remember. But the strongest memory is how her rosy cheeks and bright eyes mirrored my own exalted state – my response to the energising role of the breath and the thrill of breathing together to create that wonderful sound and feeling.

We know that matter vibrates and that different conglomerations of matter have different vibrations, so that everything resonates to its own sound. The very movement of your breath has a sound as it vibrates out into the universe. Human language and vocalising is a thing of beauty and mystery, as are the sounds made by the animals and birds.

Most ancient traditions were aware of the creative power of sound, even the sounds made when a person's breath is sounded out via the vocal cords. In ancient India, cosmic sound is said to have given rise to the whole of creation. These cosmic sounds are encapsulated in sacred syllables, each known as a *mantra*. The science of mantra says that by intoning these syllables, a person is able to align themselves with the sacred. According to an ancient Hebrew story, the universe was created by Elohim ('Source of Powers'), who spoke it into being.

The voice

The characteristic sound of our voice is generated in the larynx, or voice box. This is an organ in the throat composed of cartilage and muscle and well supplied with nerves. It is situated just below where the tract from the back of the throat splits into the trachea (the tube leading to the lungs) and the oesophagus (the tube leading to the stomach). The muscular folds in the larynx, the vocal cords, are responsible for the types of sound that we can generate. In infancy, as in most mammals, the larynx is situated high in the throat, allowing it to link more easily with the nasal passages. This ensures that breathing and eating are not done by the same organs. In adulthood the larynx descends, extending the vocal tract. This increases the variety of sounds that we can produce. The larynx is linked to the subtle energy system by the throat centre.

Our voice, via the breath, exemplifies one of the important characteristics of the human. Our voice allows us to speak, sing and say prayers. Chanting could be described as combining all three. In this chapter, we will use the breath and voice to create prayerful chants from basic sounds as well as words. The exercises encourage you to use your breath and voice to make a meaningful connection with yourself, with others, and with the source of energy and sound.

Prayer

In Hebrew, the verb to pray (*l'hit'pa'lel*) is reflexive. Prayer is something we do *to* ourselves; we pray to ourselves. The reflexive aspect of the Hebrew verb points to the mystical truth that the divine is within. This suggests that, when we pray, we are opening our consciousness to the divine within. Prayer is the world in tune, according to the seventeenth-century Welsh poet Henry Vaughan; through prayer, heaven is reflected back to us, like an echo.

The deepest purpose of prayer, then, is to move us from the mundane, through the emotional and mental levels, to the spiritual. It is another form of attunement, alignment with the sacred, or connection to the Source. We can pray silently, or we can use the breath and voice to speak, chant, or sing our prayers. In these forms, we can choose sounds that resonate with us to balance and heal ourselves or others, that express the mood of the moment, or that, when sent outward, lift up our surroundings and the world at large.

Saying prayers aloud is powerful because it resonates with the vibrations of the cosmos. At times, sacred sounds and the sounds of prayer can match the vibrations of the sounds of Creation, and every being is part of these original vibrations. In many ancient religions and cultures, such as Hinduism, Creation is regarded as the eternal now, and through breathing and chanting the sacred sounds of Creation, we reconnect with the eternal now, where all dualities are united as the One. The times of our ancestors become our times. Their moments of awakening, of awe and wonder, become our moments. When we pray out loud, we are in essence saying, 'In every moment I Am.'

Chant

According to the *Sefer Yetzirah*, a document in Kabbalah spirituality, the seemingly unusual sequence of Creation was *kol* (voice) – breath – speech. *Kol*, however, actually means 'inarticulate sound'. Thus it was the pure, non-verbal sounds that began the process of Creation. This is the rationale behind the chanting of sacred syllables, or phrases made of a series of syllables: they are creative sounds. The chanting of sacred sounds was considered a fundamental science in many ancient cultures, including ancient Egypt, and it continues to be a fundamental practice in Indian, Tibetan and Hebrew spirituality.

Sound prayer and chant have a fourfold aim. They are designed to open and develop the heart centre (as exemplified by compassion and loving kindness); to bring personal integration or wholeness to all levels of our being; to heal and remove what is preventing integration; and to reconnect us with the sacred. Essential to sound prayer, or any prayer, is our intention, and the level of our intention. Intention gives direction to our prayer. The fourfold aim of chant is achieved when the intention is to make space within us for divine energy to flow into our hearts.

Chanting has the power to restore vitality, heal and connect us to the sacred through its ability to empty us of all the energies associated with stress and anxiety. This emptiness is wholeness, a state of peace. We breathe in eternity, and we breathe out eternity. We are returned to joy.

Learning to chant begins with learning full-breath breathing. But even without any prior training, the experience of chanting positively affects our breathing. The chant exercises below encourage you to gently extend your out-breath so that your breathing becomes deeper. As you repeat the syllables of the chant, your breathing rhythm joins with the pattern of rhythmic repetition. This is why prolonged rhythmic breathing, as a consciousness-altering practice, is taught by most mystical traditions. Here, chanting is a form of meditation, or preparation for meditation.

The way we breathe is fundamental to the way we feel in our body and the way we feel emotionally and mentally. The repetitive nature of chanting encourages deeper, slower and more rhythmic breathing. The vibrations caused by making the vocal sounds resonate through-out our bodies, down to cellular level. Muscle tension relaxes, heart-beat slows and blood pressure decreases. We experience a deepening state of relaxation as well as heightened awareness. Thus, regular practice of full-breath breathing, through chanting, can create the re-laxation response and reduce stress. This brings greater mental clarity with an accompanying expansion of all the senses. On a subtle level, the vibrations of the chanting breath encourage a greater flow of the life force throughout the system.

Many popular chants are in an ancient language that may be quite foreign to you. This can be useful for the soul often seems to speak to us in a language we do not understand. Chants and mantras invite us to bypass the mind's understanding, to feel the sound within us at the deepest level. Chanting and/or praying in a language that is ancient, or not our own, can open us up to the magical and eternal language of the soul. In addition, many ancient languages, such as Sanskrit, Pali, Hebrew, Greek and Latin, for example, carry a special resonance because of their long association with chant and prayer.

The group experience

At first there may be disparate voices, but as the chant progresses the group moves towards a common vibration. Members of the chant group may experience the disappearance of a sense of separation between themselves and the other members. At this point, everyone is breathing with the same rhythm, creating energetic communion within the Breath of Unity. All over the world, especially where there is the direst poverty, people get together and sing. This means they breathe together and breathing together builds community, just as breathing together strengthens couples.

From a healing perspective, chant is the vocalisation of healing energy as well as being audible breath. The vocalisation expresses the joy of life, our Oneness with the Source and all that is, and gratitude for what healing power may bring to us, our community and the rest of the Earth family. Some of the chant exercises below, which express aspects of healing such as peace and harmony, may be used to direct these aspects to others.

The sound of silence and breathing

Follow all sound work or chanting by sitting and resting in the silence – sitting and resting in the effect of the vocalisation and chanting breath on your whole being. This achieves the ultimate purpose of the chant: to align yourself with the healing energies of the Source, via the Breath of Unity. As the German mystic Meister Eckhart (c.1260–1327) remarked, 'Nothing in the universe is so like God as silence.'

As you sit with the silence and continue with your slow and gentle full-breath breathing, see if you can sense the energy generated by the chant in the space around you and inside your own body. Allow this feeling to open you to the healing presence of the divine. Use your healing journal to record your chanting experiences. Where did they take you? What did they tell you? How did they make you feel?

Preparation

It is important to prepare the voice and body for chanting and sound prayer. Warming-up exercises are the equivalent of tuning an instrument so that it is ready to play at its best.

EXERCISE 42

Preparing yourself for chanting and prayer

The first part of preparation is to feel totally relaxed and centred.

- Sit comfortably so that the two girdles of the pelvis and shoulders are in line. Your spine should be straight and your belly relaxed. Hold your head up without straining. Rest your hands, palms up, on your thighs. If you are sitting in a chair, place your feet flat on the floor in order to feel your connection with the ground. This is your connection with the Earth. (If you are sitting cross-legged on the floor, this same connection is made via your base centre.)

- Using your breath, relax your body. With each out-breath, feel yourself gradually sinking into your pelvis.

- Relax your shoulders and the back of your neck. With each out-breath, let go of any anxieties or troubling thoughts, breathing out through your mouth. When you feel you have let go of any mental and emotional tension, close your mouth.

- Close your eyes, while remaining totally alert.

- Breathe naturally, through the nose. Keep your mouth lightly closed, with your jaw unclenched.

- Breathe gently into your abdomen and enjoy the feeling of being relaxed yet alert. Whenever you are in sitting posture, this is the ideal state to achieve.

EXERCISE 43

Preparing the voice and body for chanting

The second part of preparation is to warm up the voice and energise the body.

- Maintain your comfortable, relaxed sitting position. Breathe into your belly and on the out-breath say 'MMMM...', as if savouring the first bite of something delicious. Repeat: 'MMMM.'

- Choose a note to sing to. Breathe in slowly and deeply. With your out-breath sing a long 'MMMM' on the chosen note.

- Breathe in slowly and deeply. On the out-breath say 'AHHH...', as if experiencing the first wave of a pleasurable sensation.

- Choose a note to sing to. Breathe in slowly and deeply. With your out-breath sing a long 'AHHH' on the chosen note.

- Breathe in slowly and deeply. On the out-breath say a loud 'OH!' as if surprised.

- Choose a note to sing to. Breathe in slowly and deeply. With your out-breath sing a long 'OH' on the chosen note.

- Breathe in slowly and deeply. On the out-breath shout 'HEY!' as if to get someone's attention.

- Choose a note to sing to. Breathe in slowly and deeply. With your out-breath sing a long 'HEY' on the chosen note.

- Breathe in slowly and deeply and growl like an angry animal.

- Breathe in slowly and deeply and howl like an animal.

- Breathe in slowly and deeply and make the sound 'SHHH...' to bring silence. Start loudly and tail off your sound into silence.

exercise continues ▶

Any laughter at the end of this warming-up session is highly appropriate and welcome. Once Exercises 42 and 43 have been mastered, they can be practised as one complete preparation exercise.

The heart centre is the balance point of the subtle energy system. Like all the centres, it resonates to a particular sound. This is the long vowel AH. The next exercise helps you discover this for yourself. When you sing this tone you will experience greater resonation in the heart centre than that generated by other tones.

EXERCISE 44

The sound of the heart centre

- Maintain your previous comfortable, relaxed position. Place one hand over your heart centre (the centre of your chest). Place the fingertips of your other hand gently over the voice box (larynx) in your throat.

- Breathe in slowly and deeply. On your out-breath sing 'AH' with a strong, full voice. As you sing the tone, release the breath slowly, via your mouth, first from your belly, then from the bottom of your chest up to the top. Note which parts of you – your chest or throat – vibrated with the sound.

- With your hands in the same places, breathe in slowly and deeply. Now sing the syllable 'EE' with a strong, full voice. Again, note which parts of you – your chest or throat – vibrated with the sound.

- You should have found that 'AH' vibrates in the chest. This vibration diminishes when you sing 'EE' and you pick up the 'EE' vibration in your throat.

exercise continues ▶

- Close your eyes and bring your awareness to your breathing. As you breathe naturally, rest in the silence for one or two minutes. Use your breathing to relax your body.

- Become aware of the space between your in-breath and your out-breath, and the space between your out-breath and your in-breath. This pause is the gateway to the subtle levels and energetic input from the Source.

- As you exhale, again, make the sound 'AH', the sound that resonates with your heart centre. Make your 'AH' sound out as long as possible, without straining. Continue the sound for as long as you feel comfortable with it.

The exercise opens the heart centre, bringing energetic balance to all levels of your being. It may be practised standing or sitting, solo or with a group.

When any intentional sound is repeated for three or four minutes it becomes a chant. Chanting in this way encourages full-breath, deep-belly breathing. By controlling the air so that it is breathed out gradually, your breathing unites you with the chant. To gain the full benefit from the chants that follow, extend your sounding to five minutes each. Work with only one or two in a session, with plenty of time for silent contemplation. Use your healing journal to record the effects and inspirations that come from chanting the Breath of Unity.

EXERCISE 45
Chant – Return

This chant carries the resonance of your decision to return to, or realign yourself with, the sacred. It may be practised standing or sitting, solo or with a group. In a group setting, the chant lends itself to being a round, but the intention is not to find harmonies.

exercise continues ▶

With group chant, a harmony is reached without trying. Chant the words or invent a simple tune to fit a rhythm that you find comfortable.

- Use your breathing to relax your body. Bring your awareness to your breathing.

- Place your attention in your sacral centre (between the base of your spine and your navel). Breathe into and out from this centre three times.

- With your next breath, begin the chant. Chant the lines until you feel your breathing rhythm has completely integrated with the rhythm of the words.

- Continue the chant for as long as you feel comfortable with it.

    Return, return, return to who you are.

    Return, return, to the place of your soul.

    Return, return, to the place of your birth.

    Return, return, return.

EXERCISE 46

The Chant of the Heart for self-healing

Here the sound 'AH' is chanted or sung and your intention is to open your heart centre and energy field to receive healing, recalling that this intention will address your whole being and not simply a specific condition alone. In this way, you also open the etheric level of your energy field to receive the subtle vibrations of your breath and your own voice. It may be practised standing or sitting. This exercise is a fine introduction to sound healing.

- Close your eyes and bring your awareness to your breathing. As you breathe naturally, rest in the silence for one or two minutes. Use your breathing to relax your body.

exercise continues

- Become aware of the space between your in-breath and your out-breath, and the space between your out-breath and your in-breath.

- Focus on your heart centre and then allow your attention to spread out to the whole of your body. Rest your attention on your entire body for a few moments.

- As you exhale, sing or chant the sound 'AH'. Breathe in and exhale again, singing the same note without focusing on it. If the note needs to change during your chant, this will happen without your thinking about it. Because your focus is in the heart centre, you are making contact with your higher self. This means that the first note you unconsciously choose will

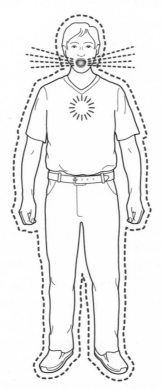

Figure 13: The Chant of the Heart for self-healing

exercise continues ▶

resonate with the part of you that needs healing. If your note changes quite spontaneously, the healing has moved to where it is needed.

- Chant the sound 'AH' as long as possible, without straining. Continue chanting for as long as you feel comfortable with it. Your healing session will come to a close quite naturally.

- Sit with the silence that follows the chant for at least two minutes before you resume other activities.

It is well known in the world of therapy that in healing others we heal ourselves. The next exercise shows how to use chanting to heal another.

EXERCISE 47

The Chant of the Heart for healing others

In this exercise, the sound 'AH' is again chanted or sung. As in the previous two exercises, this exercise opens your heart centre and the energy field around it, this time to help you heal another person. Your healing intention is conveyed by your breath and voice. With this intention, the sound 'AH' opens up the etheric level of another person to receive healing and the subtle vibrations of your breath and voice. Your intention will ensure that the vibrations of the chant will address the whole person, including any condition that may require healing. When working with a partner or a group for this purpose, have the person receiving the healing lie comfortably on the ground or on a couch with a support for the head. If necessary they can use a blanket to maintain body warmth. In this situation, the person lying down just has to relax and breathe normally without taking part in the chant.

- Stand or sit comfortably near the person to whom you are going to give healing.

exercise continues ▶

- Close your eyes if this aids your concentration. Become aware of your breathing. As you breathe naturally, rest in the silence for one or two minutes. Use your breathing to relax your body.

- Become aware of the space between your in-breath and your out-breath, and the space between your out-breath and your in-breath. This is the gateway to the subtle levels.

- Focus on your heart centre for a few moments and then move your attention to the person lying down.

- Your intention is to use the sound 'AH' in a healing mode. You will need to chant 'AH' as if singing it to the person.

- As you exhale, sing or chant the sound 'AH'. Breathe in and exhale again, keeping the same note without focusing on it.

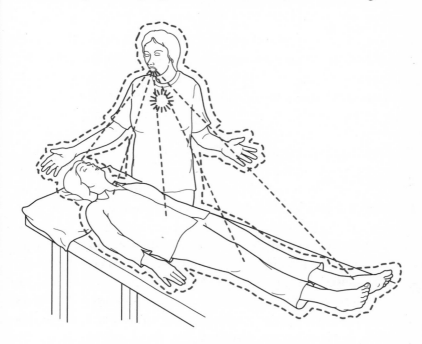

Figure 14: The Chant of the Heart for healing others.
Note the joining of the energy fields

exercise continues ▶

If the note needs to change during your chant, this will happen without your thinking about it. (If working with a small group, do not try to harmonise with the others' singing. Harmony will occur quite naturally.) As in the previous exercise where you were working on yourself, your heart centre focus ensures that you make contact with your higher self. This means that the first note you unconsciously choose will resonate with the part of the person that needs healing. The first note you choose indicates where healing is needed. If your note changes quite spontaneously, the healing has again moved to where it is needed.

- Chant the sound 'AH' as long as possible, without straining. Continue chanting for as long as you feel comfortable with it. Your healing session will come to a close quite naturally. (In a group situation, wait for the last person to finish chanting.)

- Stand or sit with the silence that follows the chant for at least two minutes. This exercise has great healing power. Help the person lying down to get up, and check that their eyes are focusing normally before you resume other activities.

EXERCISE 48

Chant – HEY YAH

Any 'calling out' activity, like the next chant, invites spirit helpers and teachers to participate in what we are doing. This very ancient Native American chant, like many other chants world-wide, is composed of vocalised sounds, or 'vocables'. These allow the chanter to use whatever pitch or tone is right for the occasion or mood of the moment. The short sound 'HEY' calls upon the Source to be with the chanter. The long sound 'YAH' points to the heart of the Source, known as the Great Mystery.

exercise continues ▶

Remembering that every breath links us to the Great Mystery, the intention behind this chant is to balance the emissive ('masculine') with the receptive ('feminine') energy streams in the body by vocalising the sounds 'HEY' and 'YAH', respectively.

Practise the two sounds until you find a tone and pitch that resonates for you. You can practise this chant while standing or sitting, solo or with a group. When practising with a group, no attempt should be made to harmonise with each other, but the group could be divided so that each grouping takes a portion of the chant. This results in a call-and-response chant. The rhythm should be slow and swaying.

- Use your breathing to relax your body. Become aware of your breathing.

- Put your mind in your heart centre (in the centre of your chest). Breathe into and out from this centre three times.

- Recall the link between your heart centre and the energy centres in each of your palms. Visualise a triangle of light, with the three points comprising your palms and your heart centre.

- The energy channels linking your palms with your shoulders carry the energies of your two energy streams: the receptive on the left side of your body, and the emissive on your right side. Visualise a triangle of light joining your two shoulders with your heart centre.

- Return your attention to your heart centre. Breathe into this centre.

- With your next breath, begin the chant. In the second line of the chant, make 'YAH' the same length as 'HEY, HEY'. Chant until you feel your breathing rhythm has completely integrated with the rhythm of the words.

- Continue the chant for as long as you feel comfortable with it.

  HEY, YAH…

  HEY, HEY, YAH…

EXERCISE 49

Chanting OM

This ultimate celebration of the Source is today a universal chant. OM is the sacred Sanskrit syllable said to be the cosmic sound giving rise to all creation. It is also used as a word for Brahman (the Sanskrit word meaning Sacred Oneness, or God). In the Hindu tradition, OM is actually the sound 'AUM'. It is made by opening the mouth wide to make a long A (*AH*) that emerges from the back of the throat. The sound continues forward through U (*OO* with rounded lips) until you gradually close the lips on the sound of M, which becomes an extended hum. Thus it is said to include all the sounds that can be made by the human voice. A second way to chant OM is to begin with the sound 'OH' (with rounded lips to make the long *O* heard in Latin languages) and end with the humming sound of M.

- Sit in a meditation position (either in a chair or cross-legged on the floor) with your hands resting on your thighs, palms facing upwards. Straighten your back and neck and make yourself comfortable.

- Take three full breaths, relaxing your body with each out-breath.

- On your next full breath, intone the sound syllable 'OM'. Pay attention to the whole of the sound from beginning to end.

- Again, breathe in and intone 'OM' with your out-breath, extending the sound for as long as is comfortable.

- Keep up the chant for five minutes, extending this to ten minutes when you feel at ease with the chant.

- Once you are proficient in following the OM, place you attention on your brow centre. Visualise that you can breathe into your brow centre, and chant 'OM' as you breathe out through

exercise continues

your brow centre, extending the sound for as long as is comfortable. Chanting OM in this way activates the brow centre and you may sense a vibration there.

- Focus on the whole of the sound from beginning to end. Once you are proficient in following the OM, imagine the sound being absorbed by your brow centre as you breathe in. As you breathe out, visualise the sound emerging from the brow centre.

- Chanting 'OM' for more than five or so minutes will encourage you to go 'out-of-body'. Allow yourself time to fully return to your body before resuming other activities. You can encourage your return by opening your eyes, wiggling your toes and rubbing your hands together.

Extending the time that you chant is effectively an advanced meditation technique in which you combine your breath with the power of sound vibration. One of the long-term benefits of this practice is that you gain greater access to intuitive wisdom and subtle sensing.

Chanting for Peace

The creation of peace and the intention towards peace are impulses from our higher self. When the word 'Peace' is capitalised, it celebrates an aspect of the Source, like the words 'Light' and 'Love'. Like all such aspects, deep and universal peace is another facet of self-healing needed by all of us if we are to live full lives and if we are to express the divine within through our lives.

In the Middle Eastern tradition, peace is not the absence of war. When someone vocally wishes you 'peace', they are extending their breath towards you to wish you peace on all levels of your being – they are wishing you total wholeness. This is the meaning of the Arabic *salaam* and the Hebrew *shalom*. Having inner peace is being consciously aware that you are complete. When you feel at peace, you feel inner completeness.

EXERCISE 50

Chant – Shalom

The intention behind chanting Shalom is to give a blessing of peace to oneself, others, and the world. Think of the word as having two sound components: 'SHA' and 'LOM', with a slight emphasis on the second syllable. SHA has a long 'A' sound; the 'OM' in LOM sounds like the 'OM' from the OM chant, with the 'M' like a final hum.

- Close your eyes and place your awareness on your breathing. As you breathe naturally, rest in the silence for one or two minutes. Use your breathing to relax your body.

- Become aware of the space between your in-breath and your out-breath, and the space between your out-breath and your in-breath.

- Put your attention in your heart centre. Breathe into this centre. As you exhale, chant the sound 'SHA...LOM'.

- Sound each component of the word as long as possible, without straining. Continue the chant for as long as you feel comfortable with it.

- Complete the chant by singing or saying the English words 'PEACE, PEACE, PEACE TO EVERY LEVEL OF YOUR BEING'.

- Now rest in the special silence that your chanting has created.

Beauty

For many people, beauty is an expression or sign of sacred presence. Natural beauty has the power to remind us of the sacred, just like the Breath of Unity. Beauty (*hózhó*) expresses the Navajo concept of sacred unity, which includes health, harmony and happiness as essentially the normal pattern of nature and life. Beauty, the presence of the divine, is generated from within us and projected out into the world. Thus, Beauty is an active and creative expression of the Breath of Unity. The capitalised word 'Beauty' is a wonderful way of referring to the Oneness, grace, and charm of All That Is. The following chant celebrates the Breath of Unity as a vehicle for Beauty, and it can also be used in any situation where Beauty has been disrupted, as in the destruction of a natural environment or the abuse of an animal, for example.

EXERCISE 51

Navajo Beauty Prayer

This chanting form of prayer is typical of the Native Americans of the Southwest. The prayer is one of acknowledgement and thanks in which the concept of wholeness as Beauty is extended out into sacred creation. The chant uses the vocalisation power of the breath to wish this aspect of the Source to be totally present for oneself and all those listening. If possible, practise the exercise while standing barefoot outdoors.

- Stand with your legs shoulder-width apart and your arms hanging loosely by your sides. Bring your arms forward a little, with the palms held upward, in a gesture of thanks and prayer.

- Take three full breaths. Pay attention to your breathing and your surroundings. Notice any other sounds that may be there to accompany you.

- Say each line of the prayer chant as you exhale. With each line, breathe in slowly.

- Breathe in. Exhale with the words: 'This prayer begins in Beauty.'

- Breathe in. Exhale with the words: 'This day arrives in Beauty.'

exercise continues ▶

- Breathe in. Exhale with the words: 'Beauty protects me.'

- Breathe in. Exhale with the words: 'My prayer protects me.'

- Breathe in. Exhale with the words: 'May I live in Beauty.'

- Breathe in. Exhale with the words: 'May I think in Beauty.'

- Breathe in. Exhale with the words: 'May I speak in Beauty.'

- Breathe in. Exhale with the words: 'May I act in Beauty.'

- Breathe in. Exhale with the words: 'Beauty before me.'

- Breathe in. Exhale with the words: 'Beauty behind me.'

- Breathe in. Exhale with the words: 'Beauty all around me.'

- Breathe in. Exhale with the words: 'I walk in Beauty.'

- Breathe in. Exhale with the words: 'This prayer is finished in Beauty.'

Once you have memorised the words of this chant, try coordinating your breathing with a soundless praying of this chant within. Or send your prayer out to the world, to your surroundings, to a place or person of your choice. The Navajo Beauty prayer can bring you feelings of peace, gratitude and oneness with the world. By chanting the prayer aloud, the voice and the breath combine to create an energetic effect that is very positive for the body and the subtle energy system.

Think about making chant a part of your daily routine. By sounding the chants above, through the breath, you manifest their energies on all levels, including the physical. Just as the beauty of the natural world, or the Earth family, awakens us to the presence of the divine, the exercises of the next chapter remind us that, as we breathe, the breath can help us link with, celebrate and honour the Earth family and the elemental components of its creation.

Chapter 10

Your breathing environment and the sacred

Breathing as natural rhythm

Life does not simply depend on the exchange of oxygen and carbon dioxide. Many members of the sulphur bacteria group, for example, do not need oxygen to live, yet they are life forms. Breathing in life forms, then, is more about the exchange of gases, not which particular gases are involved. But the rhythm of our breathing does link us to all the other natural rhythms in nature.

Life actually originates at a subtle level with the life force. We know that all life forms depend on the cycle of receiving and giving out the life force, but communication with so-called non-living aspects of nature, such as earth, rocks, rivers, seas and weather, tells us that, in fact, the life force circulates throughout all matter. The subtle energetic cycle of the life force is another natural rhythm.

If we accept the broader concept of breathing as natural rhythm, rather than simple gaseous exchange, it could help us understand and embrace our Oneness with 'all living things and the whole of the natural world in its beauty' (as Albert Einstein put it). The Breath of Unity, our moment-by-moment link with the Source, and the very rhythm of our breathing, each become the sum of all the great creative cycles of life.

Every part of the Earth family is taking in, or absorbing, different energies, even the mineral world. For example, rocks take in light, heat and infra-red and ultra-violet rays from the Sun. These energies are later released, or emitted, by the rocks. Some rocks, such as granite, emit nuclear radiation. Thus there is an energetic cycle in constant process. All things are engaged in energetic cycles and these are natural rhythms. It so happens that most plants and animals are engaged in the gaseous energy exchange that we term 'breathing'. This is a recognisable part of a whole set of natural rhythms that are the ever-changing cyclic expression of creation itself. These are the natural rhythms of taking in, absorbing, processing and then giving out.

Our relationship with the planet and planetary breathing

After leaving school, I worked on a farm, and it was there that, through intuitive, or subtle, sensing I discovered how the land breathed and how each field seemed to have its individual breath. Through intuition I was aware of the planet as a living, breathing being. This was especially true at night when I had to check on a cow that was due to calve. As I walked below the stars, I became aware of how as the land slumbered other creatures were awake and breathing. A cow's breath is sweet, calm and deep. When giving birth, she regulates her breathing rhythm to facilitate new life, to align with the rhythm of the calf that is trying to push its way out of her. We call planet Earth: Mother. She, too, regulates her breath to facilitate the myriad processes of life.

Your environment is wherever you are at any given moment. You are always somewhere on planet Earth, and you are part of the environment of the planet. Whatever you are doing, and wherever you are, your breathing is having an effect on your local environment and the planet as a whole. Just as a mother regulates her breath when giving birth, the planet is in the process of regulating its breathing to give birth to a human being who will be compatible with the spiritual evolution of the planet.

When we celebrate our deep connection with our home planet, through our breathing, we are keeping the connection alive. This is the motivation of the Aboriginal songlines: the way of walking long distances over the ground, on pathways only apparent to subtle sensing. As they walk, the people use the Breath of Unity, via chant and song, to keep the connection between Earth and Heaven. When an individual practises conscious breathing, which this book shows you how to do, it supports the breathing and well-being of the whole Earth. This chapter will help you become more aware of your relationship with the Earth, and this positive awareness will be something that you can offer to the animal, plant and mineral worlds, and the subtle dimensions of these worlds. To begin, we'll look at ways of developing a new connection with our home planet.

EXERCISE 52

Surrounding the Earth with a sphere of love

This exercise allows you to make a direct and loving contact with the Earth and its energy field through coordinating your power to visualise with your breathing. In this way, you use the power of the mind and the breath to honour and protect our home planet.

- Stand on the ground with your feet bare, if possible, shoulder-width apart. Use your breath to relax your body.

- Put your awareness in the soles of your feet. Feel your contact with the ground – the body of the Earth – and with the grass, soil, sand, or whatever is under your feet.

- Breathe in the light of the Sun, imagining that it is the light of the cosmic Sun (the Light behind the universe), into your solar plexus centre. Allow the energy to fill all parts of your body.

- Continue breathing in this vital energy until you feel totally energised.

- Now visualise that you are breathing in pink energy (the colour of unconditional love) into your heart centre. Breathe it in slowly and gently, allowing it to fill up your entire body.

exercise continues ▶

- On the next out-breath, send this energy of love to all beings in front of you with the thought, 'I give love to all beings before me.' Allow it to flow out from you, over the place where you live and out over your country, extending as far as your imagination will allow.

- Breathe in again, and on the out-breath send the energy of love to all beings behind you, with the thought, 'I give love to all beings behind me.' Breathe in again, and on the out-breath send the energy of love to the left of you, with the thought, 'I give love to all beings to the left of me.'

- Breathe in, and on the out-breath send the energy of love to the right of you, with the thought, 'I give love to all beings to the right of me.'

- You have now created an energetic circle of light that extends all around you.

- Breathe in again, and on the out-breath send the pink energy of love to all beings above you. Send your breath with the thought, 'I give love to all beings above me.'

- Breathe in once more and on the out-breath send the energy of love to all beings below you, with the thought, 'I give love to all beings below me.' Visualise the pink light extending far below and far above you. You have become the centre of a pink sphere of love energy that extends from you in all directions.

- Now visualise planet Earth in your mind's eye, as if from space, enclosed in your sphere of pink love energy.

You may wish to send this energy to parts of the planet that you feel need your extra help. For example, if you know there is trouble in a certain place, visualise this area on the surface of the planet and bathe it in the energy of love as you breathe out this intention. The energy first benefits the etheric level of the planet, and then it is 'breathed in', or absorbed, at the physical level of the planet where it is able to provide further benefit.

The seven directions

In some indigenous traditions, the four compass points of the planet are often known as the four directions. Long before the invention of the compass, these directions had been understood by our distant ancestors as related to the passage of the sun: from its rising in the east to its setting in the west, so that north was the only direction where the Sun did not appear. The four winds are the sacred breaths of the four directions. The nomadic Taureg people of the West African deserts acknowledge the tradition of the four planetary directions with beautifully wrought silver jewellery in the shape of a cross. This jewellery is handed down through the generations with the phrase: 'I give you the four directions.' However, in many traditions, seven directions are recognised. Among the Native Americans, for example, the seven directions are East, South, West, North, Above, Below and Within. The four directions are joined with the dimensions of Heaven (the Above, spiritual), Earth (the Below, physical) and Within (the indwelling soul).

To celebrate our awareness of the directions, the next exercise is based on the Buddhist practice of sending the energy of Peace out into the world by vocalising a blessing via the breath. (Peace, when capitalised, is another word for the Source.)

EXERCISE 53

Sending Peace to the seven directions

The exercise also helps make us aware of how we breathe in the seven directions and breathe out to them. It may be practised standing or sitting, indoors or outside.

- Face the direction of the dawn, the place of the rising sun (East). Use your breath to relax your body. Become aware of your feet and their contact with the ground. Feel your connection to the Earth.

exercise continues ▶

- Give thanks for the previous night. Be aware that the source of Peace, and the promise of each day, is within you.

- Feel the air around you. Become aware of your breath and the fresh air entering your nostrils and your lungs. Note how your whole body enjoys the breath of the new day.

- As you breathe slowly and naturally, raise your hands in front of you, with your elbows bent and palms facing upwards.

- In this position of prayer, you will take seven deep breaths down into your abdomen. As you exhale, you send the energy of Peace out into the world, with the spoken phrase: 'I send Peace to all beings…' and you add one of the relevant directions. Thus, carry out the exercise as follows:

- With your first breath, exhale with the phrase: 'I send Peace to all beings before me.'

- With your second breath, exhale with the phrase: 'I send Peace to all beings behind me.'

- With your third breath, exhale with the phrase: 'I send Peace to all beings to the right of me.'

- With your fourth breath, exhale with the phrase: 'I send Peace to all beings to the left of me.'

- With your fifth breath, exhale with the phrase: 'I send Peace to all beings above me.'

- With your sixth breath, exhale with the phrase: 'I send Peace to all beings below me.'

- With your seventh breath, exhale with the phrase: 'I send Peace to the being within.'

- Stay with the silence of harmony for a few moments before resuming your other activities.

Breathing green

The last exercise reconnected you to the energy web of the planet. The current and essential need for healing stems from the disruption of subtle energetic flow within the environment, as well as the millions of disconnections in the energy web that links the Earth with humans and the rest of the Earth family. One of the single most devastating causes of the disrupted energy flow is our sense of separation from the natural world. This has resulted in the breakdown of our relationship with planet Earth. This disconnection allows us to do harmful things to the environment without a second thought. When we heal the disconnection, we heal ourselves.

Both plant and animal forces are doing their best to address the imbalance caused by human activities. Plants, animals and the environment are even sending healing to us on the etheric level, but our switch to an eco-friendly lifestyle, and our own healing, is what they need. 'Breathing green' means to be aware, as we breathe, of our dependence on the natural world. This can also be your intention when you practise Exercise 29 (Thinking green, breathing green) on page 125.

The network of consciousness

From a healing point of view, the Source, the Creator, is the source of consciousness and the source of all energy. Thus, there are networks of consciousness flowing throughout the natural world, connecting everything – inorganic as well as organic.

The networks of consciousness also allow us to communicate with every cell in our body. This communication takes place on a regular basis, but we are usually quite unconscious of this. Deepak Chopra has described the network as an inner intelligence, the ultimate and supreme genius that mirrors the wisdom of the universe.

Billions of consciousness networks exist throughout the universe. Each network is breathing in the sense that rhythmic cycles of energy move to and from the members of the network. Indigenous cultures have been in touch with these networks for many thousands of years, and anthropologists have referred to this awareness as 'shamanic consciousness'. More recently, the visionary and clairvoyant ecologist Dorothy Maclean made similar discoveries in her work with plants and aspects of landscape (see her *To Honor the Earth*, for example). In her transactions with members of these worlds, she was assured that most humans are able to communicate with their environment if they become open-minded enough to do this.

Breathing with the Sun

It is thought that all the elements found on our planet originated with the explosion of the nearest star – the Sun. This star continues to provide for life on Earth. One of the vital elements it provides is light. We begin our healing connection with the breathing environment by forming a relationship with the life-giving Sun through the simple act of walking and breathing the seven rays of the light spectrum.

This book's second walking exercise is said to have been taught by Tantric masters for at least a thousand years. The exercise works with the energy centres to expand the benefits of conscious breathing during the activity of walking. The light of the Sun is breathed in as seven separate colours to balance and energise the energy centres of the body.

EXERCISE 54
Walking and breathing in the Sun

The exercise is best practised outdoors, preferably away from traffic. It does not have to be a sunny day; if it is cloudy, take notice of where the Sun would be at the time of this exercise.

• First, get used to walking at a relaxed pace and notice the way you are breathing. Next, try walking at different speeds and in different ways. What happens to your breathing?

• Introduce a breathing rhythm to your favourite way of relaxed walking. Inhale to a count of four. Hold for a count of two.

exercise continues ▶

Exhale for a count of six. Hold for a count of two. Inhale again for a count of four. And so on.

- When you feel used to this simple rhythm, exhale to a count of eight. Check that your breathing rhythm and your walking rhythm are in harmony with each other.

- Now direct your walk so that you are walking towards the Sun. You are going to use your new breathing rhythm of 4-2-8-2. Focus on your base energy centre and the colour red. Imagine that you can breathe the light of the Sun into your base centre as the colour red. Do this to a count of four. Hold for two. Exhale to a count of eight. Hold for two as you focus on your sacral centre and the colour orange.

- In time with your walking, breathe the light of the Sun into your sacral centre as the colour orange. Inhale to a count of four. Hold for two. Exhale to a count of eight. Hold for two as you focus on your solar plexus centre and the colour golden yellow.

- Breathe the light of the Sun into your solar plexus centre as the colour golden yellow. Inhale to a count of four. Hold for two. Exhale to a count of eight. Hold for two as you focus on your heart centre and the colour green.

- Breathe the light of the Sun into your heart centre as the colour green. Inhale to a count of four. Hold for two. Exhale to a count of eight. Hold for two as you focus on your throat centre and the colour sky-blue.

- Breathe the light of the Sun into your throat centre as the colour sky-blue. Inhale to a count of four. Hold for two. Exhale to a count of eight. Hold for two as you focus on your brow centre and the colour royal blue or indigo.

- Breathe the light of the Sun into your brow centre as the colour royal-blue or indigo. Inhale to a count of four. Hold for two.

exercise continues ▶

Exhale to a count of eight. Hold for two as you focus on your crown centre and the colour violet or bright purple.

- Keeping in time with your walking rhythm, breathe the light of the Sun into your crown centre as the colour violet or bright purple. Inhale to a count of four. Hold for two. Exhale to a count of eight. Hold for two as you focus on the light around your body. Imagine that this is a golden light.

- Return to your relaxed walking, knowing that you are now fully energised.

In the previous exercise, the prismatic rays represent the light of the cosmic Sun, or divine Light. By breathing in the light, you are said to become one with the Source of light. Here, the light is your partner.

The aim of all Tantric Yoga is union: union with the Source, or union with one's partner, who represents the Source. Even lovemaking is practised as a sacred ritual where each sees the other as a form of the divine. The central scripture of Tantra, the Mahanirvana Tantra, counsels that both partners should learn to blend their breathing to create a single breathing rhythm at all stages of the ritual.

Through blending your breathing rhythm with the rhythms you encounter in the exercises, you engage in a profound self-healing process that is a true form of loving oneself and the higher self. The rhythm of all forms of breathing teaches us about relationship.

Communicating with the elements

Communication with the elements begins by acknowledging our relationship with them. We need to make sure that we can open our lines of communication with the Earth and the Earth family. The unbalanced state of our subtle energy system mirrors that of the planet and our need for the right relationship with the Earth begins here. Like the planet, we are all composed of the four essential elements of life on the physical level. The body is linked to the element Earth and the base centre. The various fluids of the body are linked to the element Water and the sacral centre. The heat of the body is linked to the element Fire and the solar plexus centre. Our breath is linked to the element Air, the life force, and the heart centre. Because of our elemental make-up, we can see that what happens to the planet is energetically reflected in us, and what happens to us is mirrored in the state of the planet. This is what you will discover when you open your lines of communication with your environment.

We are one with the Sun and Fire. The life of the Sun is our life. Every time that we work with the Sun in a sacred manner, we do something to bring harmony to the human heart and to return warmth to human relationships. We are one with the rivers, rain and seas. When we work with Water in a sacred manner, we do something to bring harmony to human emotions and send a message to encourage the purification of all forms of water. We are one with the Earth. When we work with the Earth in a sacred manner, we do something to bring harmony to the human body and respect for the mineral world from which our bodies are composed. We are one with Air. Its life is our life. The state of air on the planet reflects the state of human thought. Every time that we work with Air in a sacred manner (such as with conscious breathing), we do something to bring harmony to human thinking and to return purity to the Air.

The next exercises in this chapter, with the elements of Water and Air, not only help you to acknowledge your link with these elements, they help you to reconnect with them and to look at how they compose the natural world around you. You can begin in a simple way by becoming aware of the climate, the movement of air and water, the ground beneath your feet, the features of the landscape and the signs of the seasons. Even in the middle of a city, your home is rooted in Nature and depends on it. You drink water, you eat the food that was grown somewhere, and you breathe the air of the city.

We need air to breathe, but this simple view of air's purpose has a long history. Empedocles, the fifth-century BCE Greek philosopher, scientist and healer, developed the theory of the Four Elements. He stated that there are four basic components of life:

continues ▶

Earth, Fire, Water and Air. He associated the element Air with the king of the gods, Zeus, because according to his theory, Air is the key element. A hundred years later, the four classical elements were used by the 'father' of modern medicine, Hippocrates, to describe the four 'humours' of the human body. Yellow bile was related to Fire, black bile to Earth, phlegm to Water, and blood to Air. The doctrine of the four humours continued to dominate European medicine through the medieval period until the middle of the eighteenth century.

In India, a century before Empedocles presented his theory, the Buddha (c.563–c.483 BCE) taught that a concept of there being only four elements creating form in the universe was too simplistic. Matter, he taught, is composed of much smaller particles that are constantly changing. This concept proved to be far ahead of its time and, for many centuries, Greek ideas more easily matched the logic of Western scientists and physicians.

In Western astrology, which owes much to Hindu and Arab research, the four elements have survived up until the present day. The twelve signs of the zodiac are divided into groups of three, and each group is linked to one of the four elements. The three Air signs are Gemini, Libra and Aquarius. The ancient divinatory cards of the Tarot also follow the four elements, with the suit of Swords linked to Air.

The exercises give you the opportunity to commune with aspects of the environment that surround you. As you discovered in Chapter 8 (especially Exercise 35: The Breath of Connection, page 140), all communication is about making connections. Use your practice of breathing out to another person to gain the full benefit from any exercise involving communication – in all its forms.

EXERCISE 55

Communing with Air

This exercise allows you the possibility of communicating with the element we most associate with breathing and the transmission of the life force. A question you might ask is: 'Does Air have something to share with me?' If possible, practise the exercise outdoors.

- Stand barefoot on the ground with your feet shoulder-width apart and your knees gently flexed. Use your breath to relax, while remaining totally aware of your breath and your surroundings.

- Remain aware of your breathing as you breathe into your heart centre. Air carries the animating life force and the oxygen that your body needs. It also carries the waste gases that your body discards. It carries the scent of the breeze, the flowers, the trees and the sea.

- Recall a time when you simply enjoyed the feel of the open air or the wind. Even if the experience you call to mind is negative or overwhelming, allow yourself to recall it and then accept your experience.

- How is the Air moving around and through you right now? What does this feel like?

- You are communing with the element Air. Let your natural rhythm of breath be an expression of gratitude to Air. Allow Air to speak to you.

When you next perform this exercise, change your body position and/or location. Note any changes in your communion with Air.

Breathing began in water

Breathing, in the broad sense of the exchange of life-sustaining gases, began in water, not air. Beings, including plants, animals and insects, first had to adapt to the exchange of gases in water. Later, those that had moved to life on land had to adapt again to the exchange of gases in air. But water, in the form of various fluids, is still the medium for processing gaseous exchange. We still use a liquid (blood) to convey oxygen to every cell in the body. We can trace our breathing rhythm back beyond our Earthly ancestors to our ancestors in the oceans.

EXERCISE 56

Communing with Water

If possible, find a natural source of water, which can be large or small. If not, you can use a basin or glass of water. Or you can even visualise a source of water.

- Stand or sit near the water source you have chosen (or which has chosen you!). Use your breathing to relax your body.

- Become aware of your breathing, and imagine that you can breathe into the sacral centre. Breathe naturally.

- Water quenches your thirst, and the thirst of the land and plants. Recall a time being beside the ocean, or watching the movement of a stream or river, when you simply enjoyed drinking fresh water, or remember listening to the soothing sound of rain. Even if the experience you call to mind is negative or overwhelming, allow yourself to recall it and then accept your experience.

- You are communing with the element of Water. Allow Water to 'speak' to you. Feel that you can absorb what it is communicating via your sacral centre. See if you can engage in this dialogue, which may be without words. Note everything that this particular source conveys to you.

exercise continues ▶

- Close the exercise with your thanks.

The exercise allows you to link with the subtle levels of water. Practise the exercise with a different source of water. Notice any differences between, say, an ocean and a lake, a river and a tiny stream. Remember that other sources – rain, snow, ice, a waterfall – can all be engaged with.

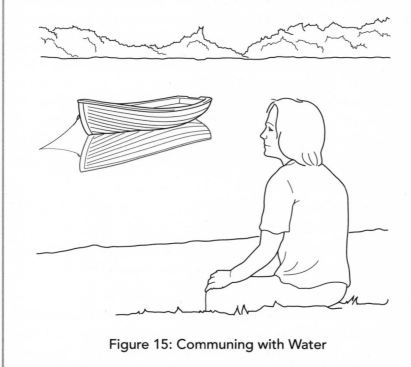

Figure 15: Communing with Water

Through the network of consciousness, the natural world has always been speaking to us. Most of the time we can appreciate its beauty, but it is easy to lose the awareness of how nature never gives up reaching out to us. The next, final exercise offers a way of honouring and completing the communication cycle of the breath.

EXERCISE 57

Breathing the energies of the natural world

If possible, practise this exercise outdoors in a place you consider especially beautiful. If you can't get outside, study a beautiful photo or picture before you begin the exercise. If you are unable to take up the bodily positions described, the exercise may still be done through your imagination. Take your time, and be prepared to spend some time absorbing each part of the total experience.

- Lie down with your back touching the ground. Your legs should be slightly apart with your feet relaxed. Let your arms relax by your sides with the palms of your hands up. Relax your body and breathe naturally.

- Placing your awareness in the ground, and the Earth that nurtures you, breathe in the energy around you through the whole surface of your body.

- While still lying on the ground, open yourself to the fact that every plant, with its roots in the soil, pushes up into the light with its growing tip. Remaining aware of your connection to the plant world, imagine that you can breathe the shimmering subtle light of plants into the tips of your fingers and toes.

- Open your awareness to the waters of the Earth and the creatures that live in them. Recall how they take in the life force that is carried by the water. As they take in the energies they need, imagine that your breathing is in time with their rhythms.

- Turn over and rest comfortably on the front of your body, with your arms bent at the elbows. Let your palms rest on the ground in line with your head. Open your awareness to the creatures that travel over the Earth; imagine that you can breathe in the light of their shimmering subtle energies into the whole back surface of your body.

exercise continues ▶

- Being aware of the creatures that live under the Earth, breathe their light energy into the whole front surface of your body.

- When you feel ready, stand up and cross your arms loosely over your heart centre. Now slowly open them, completely extending your arms out on a level with your shoulders. Being aware of all the creatures that fly, breathe their light energy into your heart centre.

- Relax your arms by your side. Make sure that your feet are shoulder-width apart with your knees gently flexed. Slowly raise your arms, with the palms facing upwards, to form a Y-shape. Open your awareness to the trees, and breathe their subtle light into your palms. Now put your attention on your 'branches', your 'trunk' and your 'roots'.

- Relax your arms by your side again. Spend some time with this experience.

You may want to illustrate your experience in some way or write about it in your healing journal. Topics you could consider are how you felt during specific inhalations. Further, did you notice any changes in your breath during the exercise?

You can follow up this exercise by recalling that each network of consciousness is able to interact with all other networks. This is possible because the subtle reality is that we are all one. If you send a prayer or chant to the rocks, they will send it out to the mountains, hills and the stones of the city. If you send a prayer or chant to a tree, the tree will send the prayer on to other trees, and to the sky. If you send a prayer or chant to a bird, the bird will send your prayer out to other birds, and to the heavens. If you send a prayer or chant to the sea, the sea will pass your prayer on to the sea creatures, and the tides of the sea will take it further. If you whisper a prayer or chant to a stream, the stream and its network will carry it to inland waters and the creatures that live there. Use the full extent of your voice and your breathing, from a whisper to a shout, to send a prayer or a chant to the world.

Your gift

To live fully we must open our awareness. Then we become more aware of the living breath of the natural world, of our body, emotions and mind, of our relationships with others and of the abiding presence of our higher selves. To energise your breathing practice and deeply enhance your life, practise breathing from the heart, because, through breathing, you acknowledge your love for and oneness with all beings. Raising your consciousness in this way raises all consciousness and pours healing out into the cosmos. Your heart knows that you do not need to get something from your breathing practice. Rather, conscious breathing is a way of being who you really are. Your breathing practice has life force when it is offered to all beings as a gift, dedicated to peace and harmony in the world. By making sure that these loving attitudes are in place, your breathing practice has great healing power for yourself, the Earth, and the Earth family.

In every breath there is a beginning and an ending. In every breath there is an opening and a closing. Staying present to your breath celebrates your truth as a spiritual being and helps prevent you from identifying solely with aspects of the physical world around you and with your mental and emotional reactions to those aspects. Within nature you will find the resonance of the Source which lies at the heart of your breath. Return to your breath, return to your sacred self, celebrate your sacred identity and breathe with a heart filled with the promise of a healthy, fulfilling life. May this celebration be your personal and collective gift to the next seven generations!

Glossary

Akasha: Sanskrit *ākāsha* (pronounce 'ā' long as in the sound 'ah'), ether, from the root *kāsh*: to radiate, shine; the basis and essence of all things; a luminous substance. See also **ether**.

All That Is: when capitalised, another term for Oneness, the Source, the Creator, which some call God. It implies that there is nothing outside Oneness and that we, all other beings, and the rest of the universe, are not separate from the Source.

Ankh: ancient Egyptian, the key of life.

Aura: the total energetic emanation of the human being, including the physical, etheric and other energy zones; the human energy field.

Awen: Welsh for, ether, wind, breeze. Used in Druidism to indicate the inspiration of the bards and poets.

Breath of Unity: The self-healing realisation that every breath can be a conscious reminder of our unity with the Source of life.

Chakra: now a common term for a subtle energy centre. From Sanskrit, *chakram* 'wheel' (pronounce with short 'a' and 'ch' as in English word 'child'). The whirling vortex of energy looks somewhat like a turning cartwheel.

Creation: when capitalised, the universe or cosmos as the physical place for the manifestation of the Source as soul, or higher self.

Earth: when capitalised, refers to our planet as a being in its own right.

Earth family: the other beings that share the Earth with us.

Energy: a force directed by, and emanating from, the Source. Spirit is the energy of the Source. Compared with this level of energy, that of the physical has a vastly lower frequency.

Energy centre: a subtle structure, detected in the etheric body, designed to allow the flow of subtle energies into and out of the human energy field. See also **chakra**.

Ether: ancient Greek, initially referring to the upper regions of the atmosphere, or heaven. Seers of the time had witnessed that, on passing over, people carried on being in their 'heavenly' or etheric body. Later, Greek seers confirmed that human beings were composed of this subtle substance which emanated, like light, an inch or so around the physical body, especially around the head.

Etheric: the energetic level next to the physical at which energy vibrates at a higher frequency. It acts as the bridging zone between the physical and the subtle and is the support system for the physical body. From the ancient Greek term *ether* which referred to the upper regions of the atmosphere, or heaven. See **ether**.

Higher self: the human soul; the indwelling spiritual force of the human being.

Life force: the vital energy, essential to life, conducted by the subtle energy system; also known as *prana* (Sanskrit), *qi* (Chinese) and *ki* (Japanese).

Light: when capitalised, another word for the Source, Oneness, or

God; an aspect of spiritual energy; a force that encourages healing and enlightenment.

Love: when capitalised, another word for the Source, Oneness, or God; a force that encourages healing and integration.

Mantra: Sanskrit, a voiced sacred syllable or series of syllables said to embody aspects of Brahman (the Source), or the myriad manifestations of the Source.

Oneness: when capitalised, another word for the Source (which some call God); a term which describes the sacred unity of All That Is.

Patient: a conventional therapeutic term which simply distinguishes the person who is receiving help from the healer.

Personality: the self; the ego; the physical consciousness of the self that tends to see itself as separate from all that is, i.e., the natural world, the higher self and the Source, or Oneness.

Polarity: the energy systems of living things, including humans, have two aspects or polarities: the receptive (often erroneously termed the feminine) and the emissive (often erroneously termed the masculine). The possibility of receiving and giving out energy ensures its cyclic nature. Human health and well-being depends on maintaining a balance between the two energy streams.

Prana: Sanskrit, *prāna* (pronounce 'ā' long as in the sound 'ah'), the life force in air and the breath; the basis of life.

Pranayama: Sanskrit, the science of working with the breath and the life force through a series of exercises; a branch of yoga.

Qi: Chinese (pronounce 'q' somewhat like a soft English 'ch', the syllable spoken with a falling tone), the life force in air and the breath, said to circulate throughout the body and the subtle energy system; the basis of life.

Self: lower case, see **Personality**.

Source: when capitalised, another term for Oneness, which some call God; the Creator; the source of all energies.

Spirit: when capitalised, another term for Oneness, which some call God; in lower case, the energy of the Source.

Subtle energy: when used in this book, energy vibrating at a higher frequency than physical matter. Such energy, travelling at a velocity beyond the speed of light, behaves in ways very different to those physical energies at present known to most science. (See William Tiller's work in the Further Reading section.)

Subtle energy medicine: any therapy that works primarily with the subtle energy system to bring balance and/or harmony to the subject. The therapeutic use of the breathing exercises in this book is such a healing modality.

Subtle energy system: the coordinated system of the etheric body, comprising the energy centres (chakras) and their etheric network links and the other zones of the energy field.

Wakhan Tanka: Lakota term. (*Wakhàn tànka*, 'h' is slightly aspirated after 'k'. Both 'n' sounds are nasal, 'à' is a long stressed 'a'.) Translated as Great Spirit, Great Mystery, Great Sacred Energy (the Source). *Wakhàn* always refers to something spiritual or sacred.

Yoga: Sanskrit, from the root *yug*, to unite or yoke. In Indian (Hindu) spirituality, systems of exercises designed to unite a person with the Atman (higher self) and Brahman (the Source), which are considered one and the same. In modern Western language, yoga refers to a system of body (Hatha Yoga) and breathing (Pranayama) exercises.

Further reading

Apart from references in the text, some of the titles below explore the breath and breathing. Others explore our relationship with the breath and breathing.

Angelo, Jack, *Your Healing Power*, London: Piatkus Books, 1994, revised edn 2009.

Angelo, Jack, *Hands-On Healing*, Rochester, VT: Healing Arts Press, 1997.

Angelo, Jack, *The Distant Healing Handbook*, London: Piatkus Books, 2007.

Angelo, Jack, *Distant Healing, A Complete Guide: How to send healing to people, animals, the environment, and around the world*, Boulder, CO: Sounds True, 2008.

Angelo, Jack and Angelo, Jan, *The Spiritual Healing Handbook: How to develop your healing powers and increase your spiritual awareness*, London: Piatkus Books, 2007.

Bailey, Alice A., *Esoteric Healing*, New York: Lucis Publishing Company and London: Lucis Press Ltd, 1993.

Campbell, Don, *The Mozart Effect*, London: Hodder & Stoughton, 2001.

Dentin, Diana, *In the Tenderness of Stone: Liberating consciousness through the awakening of the heart*, Pittsburgh, PA: Sterling House, 1998.

Dossey, Larry, *Healing Beyond the Body: Medicine and the infinite reach of the mind*, Boston and London: Shambhala Publications, 2001.

Douglas-Klotz, Neil, *The Hidden Gospel: Decoding the spiritual message of the Aramaic Jesus*, Wheaton, IL: Quest Books, 2001.

Flanagan, Sabina, *Hildegard of Bingen, a Visionary Life*, London: Routledge, 1989.

Gerber, Dr Richard, *Vibrational Medicine for the 21st Century*, London: Piatkus Books, 2000.

Govinda, Lama Anagarika, *Foundations of Tibetan Mysticism*, London: Rider, 1959.

Holy Bible: New Revised Standard Version, New York and Oxford: Oxford University Press, 1995.

Jewish Study Bible, Tanakh Translation, New York and Oxford: Oxford University Press, 2004.

Judith, Anodea, *Waking the Global Heart: Humanity's rite of passage from the love of power to the power of love*, Santa Rosa, CA: Elite Books, 2006.

Kalweit, H., *Dreamtime and Inner Space: The world of the shaman*, Boston, MA: Shambhala Publications, 1998.

Khan, Hazrat Inayat, *The Complete Sayings of Hazrat Inayat Khan*, New York: Omega Publications, 1978.

Maclean, Dorothy, *To Honor the Earth*, New York: HarperSanFrancisco, 1991.

McLuhan, T.C., *Touch the Earth: A self-portrait of Indian existence*, New York: Outerbridge & Dienstfrey, 1972.

Pecci, Ernest F. and Tiller, William A., *Science and Human Transformation: Subtle energies, intentionality and consciousness*, Walnut Creek, CA: Pavior Publishing, 1997.

Rodenburg, Patsy, *Presence*, London: Michael Joseph, 2007.

Sabatini, Sandra, *Breath: The essence of yoga – a guide to inner stillness*, London: Pinter & Martin, 2007.

Tick, Edward, *The Practice of Dream Healing: Bringing ancient Greek mysteries into modern medicine*, Wheaton, IL: Quest Books, 2001.

Tiller, William A., 'What are subtle energies?', *Journal of Scientific Exploration*, vol. 7, no. 3, 1993.

Townley, Wyatt and Dinyer, Eric, *The Breathing Field: Meditations on yoga*, Boston, New York and London: Little, Brown and Company, 2002.

Winkler, Gershon, *Magic of the Ordinary: Recovering the shamanic in Judaism*, Berkeley, CA: North Atlantic Books, 2003.

Web resources

www.caduceus.info
Caduceus magazine – 'Healing for people, community and planet' (UK)

www.circleofcompassion.org
The Circle of Compassion – 'Compassion encircles the earth for all beings' (US)

www.conscious-learning-community.com
The Conscious Learning Community, Boulder, Colorado

www.contemplativemind.org
The Center for Contemplative Mind in Society (US)

www.dosseydossey.com
Official website of Dr Larry Dossey, who has written extensively on the power of intention and intentional prayer (US)

www.hayfoundation.org
The Hay Foundation – 'Helping those who care' (US and UK)

www.issseem.org
The International Society for the Study of Subtle Energies and Energy

Medicine – a meeting place for scientists, mystics and energy
practitioners (US)

www.jackangelo.net
Website of the author, Jack Angelo – artist, writer and teacher in
the fields of subtle energy medicine, natural spirituality and world
spiritual traditions (UK)

www.miriamscyberwell.com
Ravi Miriam Maron uses chant and sound prayer in her work,
especially in teaching the shamanic basis of Judaism. Site lists
details of her work and CDs (US)

www.nccih.nih.gov
The National Center for Complementary and Alternative Medicine
(US)

www.nealedonaldwalsch.com
The work of Neale Donald Walsch and the *Conversations With
God* material

www.noetic.org
The Institute of Noetic Sciences (IONS) (US)

www.resurgence.org
Resurgence magazine – linking ecology, spirituality, art and
culture (UK)

www.sacredcenters.com
Anodea Judith and her work in chakra (energy centre) psychology
and spirituality

www.spiritualityhealth.com
Spirituality & Health magazine (US)

www.tillerfoundation.com
Website of Professor William Tiller's work

www.ukhealers.info
Association of UK healing organisations

www.wholistichealingresearch.com
Wholistic Healing Research, hosted by leading researcher
Dr Daniel Benor

Index

THE
DISTANT HEALING
HANDBOOK

*How to send healing to people, animals,
the environment and global trouble spots*

BY JACK ANGELO

The Distant Healing Handbook is an important new book from Jack
Angelo, the UK's leading teacher of healing and subtle energy medicine. Jack explains that we all have it in our power to heal, even when
hands-on healing is not possible. Distant healing enables you to take
action – to reach out and help people, places and animals who are in
need. Step-by-step, using over 60 easy-to-follow exercises, Jack shows
you how to access your own distant healing power and harness your
love and energy for the good of others.

    The Distant Healing Handbook will enable you to:

- Sense your energy field and send healing to people at any distance

- Work on your own or with a group or healing circle

- Send healing to the environment, plants and animals

- Send light to trouble spots and disaster areas around the world

- Practise unconditional love and bring healing into your
  everyday life

The Distant Healing Handbook is a book everyone can use, whether you
already have a healing gift or whether you simply want to learn how
to send healing and make a difference to a loved one, a pet or to the
world we live in.

ISBN: 978 0 7499 2815 5